DAUGHTERS OF DISSIDENTS NEED NOT APPLY

This edition was published by The Dreamwork Collective
The Dreamwork Collective LLC, Dubai, United Arab Emirates
thedreamworkcollective.com

Printed and bound in the United Arab Emirates
Cover: Nuno Moreira, nmdesign.org
Design: Kasia Piatek, kasiapiatek.pl

Text © Nadina Ronc, 2025

This book is approved by the National Media Council under the age classification E
MC-02-01-4860052

ISBN 978-9948-724-13-1

All rights reserved. No part of this publication may be reproduced, stored, or transmitted in any form or by any means, electronic, mechanical, photocopying, recording, or otherwise, without prior permission of the publishers. The right of Nadina Ronc to be identified as the author of this work has been asserted and protected under the UAE Copyright and Authorship Protection Law No. 7.

The names of some individuals, organisations, and locations in this book have been changed for privacy. Any resemblance to actual persons, living or dead, is coincidental. The opinions, experiences, and stories shared within are those of the author alone and do not necessarily reflect the views or opinions of the publisher. The publisher makes no representations or warranties regarding the accuracy of the contents.

DAUGHTERS OF DISSIDENTS NEED NOT APPLY

NADINA RONC

THE
DREAMWORK
COLLECTIVE

To Mama

"In a time of universal deceit, telling the truth is a revolutionary act."
— commonly attributed to George Orwell

PART I (1991–1993)

ROLLER SKATES

They were fluorescent green roller skates with black velvet fabric on the sides and green shoelaces, and they fitted me like a glove. I hardly took them off. They were my pride and joy. My friends and I would spend every free moment roller-skating around our L-shape apartment building in Brcko, a port city in the northeast of Bosnia and Herzegovina, where I lived with my parents and brother. We were an army of ten-year-olds on roller skates, zooming around like a little squadron of mischief-makers. Our train engines were boys on bicycles who would pull us around the building. We would sometimes not push forward, pretending we were passengers, which infuriated the boy at the helm who would shout, "PUSH! I can't pull all of you." There were over ten of us, and when we got going, the sound of all those roller skates was like a steam train leaving the station. We would go past the leather shop and the pizza restaurant, and sometimes they waved to us, pretending we were off on a journey, all while we giggled and held on to each other. But some neighbours who worked during the night didn't share the same enthusiasm. They would come onto their balconies to scold us for making noise. We'd stop briefly, give them a half-hearted, "Sorry, we'll be quiet," and exchange that classic "Shall we?" look before going right back to mischief. And it would be like that every free moment I had. I only stepped into our apartment when Mama called out for me to come in and eat or when I had homework, but as soon as that was done, I would be back to troublemaking and roller-skating.

Mama was the heart and soul of our household. She had an almost magical ability to balance everything—work, home, and family. She was an economics graduate who worked as a bookkeeper and managed our household with ease, ensuring everything ran smoothly, from my brother and me to her work and social responsibilities. Mama had a quiet strength that held us all together. Despite her busy schedule, she always made time for us, whether it was helping with homework or preparing our favourite meals. She kept my brother and me in line, but she was never strict, allowing us to enjoy our childhood. Whenever a student struggled with English classes and needed extra help to pass the year, their parents or relatives would often turn to Mama. They would ask her to speak to my father, an English language professor, on their behalf, knowing she could sway him. With her gentle persuasion, Mama would speak to my father, and he would agree to assist the student in need. Her influence was always impactful.

We lived in the second-floor apartment. It was a spacious two-bedroom apartment with a long corridor and a balcony overlooking all the mischief of my childhood. I shared my room with my brother Husein, whose friends called him Huso. Husein was two years older and a bit taller than me. He had thick brown hair and brown eyes.

Husein and I did not go to the same school. Mine was Jelenka Vockic and his Tamara Begovic. It was probably best that we went to different schools, given that we shared a room. Spending time with a sibling has its limits, but we made the most of it. When my uncle started building his country house, and we visited him, we turned the foundation into our personal racetrack. We'd zoom around the huge, empty slab like caffeinated squirrels, laughing our heads off every time we managed to tag each other. It was basically our own personal Olympic event, minus the medals but with double the chaos! We were different, Husein and I. He played football with his friends, I roller-skated with mine. I was pedantic and loved designing clothes for my Barbie dolls. As a child, I wanted to be a fashion designer, watching my dresses worn by famous models gliding on the catwalk. Later, I also wanted to be a rock star, but who didn't? When Husein played football, he was covered in mud, but when he wasn't playing outside, he was often on his Commodore 64, which he had to plug into a TV we had in our room. We regularly fought over the remote when our parents allowed us to watch TV. I used it to watch New Kids on the Block on MTV so I could torture my brother singing "Step by Step" at the top of my lungs like a patriotic rendition of a national anthem. There was also Guns N' Roses, whose music I belted out as if I were performing my own rock concert, thoroughly enjoying the fact that I was irritating Husein in the process. Although I could read a book from start to finish in one sitting, he often fell asleep with a book resting on his face.

My brother and I had a lot of friends. But I was more active in the community. I participated in local theatre productions and later sang in a choir that performed at a theatre. I remember wearing all white for one winter performance: a white above-the-knee skirt, white shirt, socks, and shoes. I don't know what the local choir was trying to achieve with that look in the dead of winter, but it worked enough to provoke many questions afterwards. It had been bitterly cold, and on the way back, even though I had a winter coat on, my brother's school friend asked him whether I had misplaced a calendar. But nothing could knock my spirit. I had performed in a local choir. And just for that moment, I may have been a rock star who loved going to school.

I was a super nerd. I still am. I had top grades, and history was my favourite class. We had a teacher called Savo, who also taught my cousin Tanja when she was in school. He was old and grumpy, looked like Gargamel from the Smurfs, and instilled a fear of God in all of us. His classes were simple. He always said, "Underline everything I read, and learn it by heart for the next class". So, he would read chapter after chapter, and we would underline them with a pencil. And may God help you if you did not learn it by heart. We probably all developed a photographic memory in his class. What choice did we have? He would randomly pick one of us to come to the front and stand next to him while he started questioning us as if we were witnesses at a trial. We always had to be correct, or it was an instant fail. His questions were random, but the answers had a story to tell.

I was also good at the English language. Of course, it helped to have a father who was a professor of it. But I hated learning English with my father because he was so strict and lost his temper quickly. What I enjoyed was reading the English books he brought from England, where he was an exchange student in the 1960s. Aside from my father being an English professor and Mama working as a bookkeeper, they also had a private business, a language school, which was a stone's throw from our apartment building. My brother and I were enrolled on the weekends, and sometimes we attended after school. Our parents planned to send us to England to university.

My parents were well known in Brcko, with the private language school and Mama's bookkeeping and my father's international experience and teaching. It seemed everyone in town had either been taught by my father or had family members in his class. His role as a local parliament member and a hobby as a court translator handling translations between Bosnian and English, added to his prominence amongst a vibrant network of friends, most of whom were doctors and company directors.

Besides my obsession with roller-skating, ten-year-old me was completely hooked on sledging. My brother and I had two sledges: One was a metal beast with a wooden seat that felt like sitting on a frozen throne, and the other was a wannabe dog-sledge, complete with a cushy seat and speed to leave a cheetah wondering where it all went wrong. I rocketed down the hill like a bat out of hell, so bundled up against the cold that I looked like a snowball with eyes. When we weren't risking life and limb on sledges, we were hurling snowballs with the accuracy of blindfolded ninjas or crafting snowmen that resembled lumpy marshmallow monsters until the light of day gave up on us. We even tried skiing down the hill on tiny, colourful skis, but let's just say I spent more time kissing the snow than skiing on it!

When I think of winter, I'm transported back to those chilly Bosnian days, blanketed in snow like a perfect Christmas postcard. But summer was truly my season. I wasn't made for the cold and eagerly anticipated our summer vacations in Croatia or Montenegro, where we'd travel with our parents. I would spend hours swimming in the Adriatic Sea, a place Husein and I loved so much that Mama often had to pull us out so we could have lunch. The beach was my paradise, especially with the endless supply of ice cream.

Aunt Rahima, my father's older sister, would sometimes join us on our vacation, and her presence meant spoiling us with a delightful surfeit of sweets, which earned me a frequent flyer status at the dentist's office in Brcko—something like VIP status, thanks to my parents' good reputation in our hometown.

Summers were filled with fun, especially when Mama and Aunt Rahima played pranks on each other. One memorable prank involved Aunt Rahima flirting with a man at a café. Mama instructed cousin Tanja, my brother, and I to call Aunt Rahima "Mama" in unison as we passed by. The man, believing the ruse, made a hasty exit, much to Aunt Rahima's amusement. She had a fantastic sense of humour and was always stylish with her wavy black hair and red lipstick, and she cherished every moment with us.

My aunt was one of seven siblings. Two passed away at birth, two in the 1980s, and then there was Uncle Huso, Aunt Rahima, and finally my father. After my grandfather, a horse trader, died of a heart attack when my father was just two years old, my paternal grandmother raised all the children alone. Despite the hardship, they were fortunate enough to be well off and lacked for nothing.

Aunt Rahima's husband, a Serb, passed away from sarcoma cancer in Heidelberg, Germany, when Tanja was just one year old. Aunt Rahima never remarried and devoted her time to spoiling us when Tanja went off to university in Sarajevo. Tanja, a mousy blonde who drank Coca Cola like her life depended on it (which was often reflected on her acne-covered face) was about fourteen years older than me, and during her breaks in June or July, she and her friends would take me to the local swimming pool. I adored those outings, and her friends always made me feel welcome.

As the holidays drew to a close and the new school year began, we continued to enjoy a remarkable sense of freedom. Even as children, we felt confident venturing to the town library on our own. In Yugoslavia, crime felt like a distant concept, and the social safety net seemed unshakeable. Walking to the library was an ordinary and cherished part of my childhood in Brcko. That library had a profound impact on my early years.

My father was always so busy, running the private school and teaching. In 1990, he became a member of the Party of Democratic Action (SDA), founded by Alija Izetbegovic who would later become the first President of an independent Republic of Bosnia and Herzegovina. After Josip Broz Tito's death in 1980, Yugoslavia began to transform. Under

Tito, the principle of "brotherhood and unity" downplayed ethnic and religious differences, fostering a unified Yugoslav identity that kept tensions in check. But after his passing, this identity weakened as religious and ethnic affiliations quietly reemerged. A form of secret segregation took hold, gradually dividing communities that had once coexisted peacefully. As these divisions grew, the shared Yugoslav identity unravelled, setting the stage for the conflicts of the 1990s and the eventual breakup of Yugoslavia, as republics sought independence.

I was born after Tito's death, so I never lived in his version of Yugoslavia, but I know from Mama that it was a time when life was good and prosperous. Security was intact, and everyone had opportunities, and the states that formed Yugoslavia were kept in line by Tito's firm rule.

After Tito's death, as nationalism and ethnic identity became more prominent, Bosnian Croats and Bosnian Serbs aligned themselves with political parties representing their ethnic groups. This period was also marked by widespread political discourse.

There probably wasn't a home in the country where political debates wouldn't regularly take place. And mine was no exception! My parents would often discuss the latest political events. I remember going with them to visit some of their friends from all ethnic backgrounds, and they would all be sitting, enjoying food and drink and talking incessantly about events in Yugoslavia, and between playing and getting a drink, I would overhear what was said. At first, I barely paid attention to the political talk swirling around me. My parents discussed it, but I didn't think much of it—until the Vukovar massacre in Croatia in 1991. That changed everything. The air around us grew heavy, conversations became urgent, no longer avoidable. I'll never forget the bus that arrived in Brcko, packed with terrified Croat civilians who had narrowly escaped the massacre. Mama and the other women rushed to help, bringing food, water, blankets, anything they could. I was too young to grasp the magnitude, but I could feel the fear, the tension. Those people were shaken to their core.

Years later, Mama told me about the stories they shared, of the bloodshed and chaos. People who were meant to be protected were slaughtered and buried in mass graves like their lives didn't matter. It was horror on a scale I couldn't imagine, and yet, those around me seemed to carry on as if nothing had changed. The denial was suffocating. How could they not see it? How could they pretend everything was still the same, when the world as we knew it was beginning to unravel?

Everything Tito had built for Yugoslavia was swept away in favour of Serbian nationalism. The dream of a Greater Serbia, which dated back to 1844 when Ilija Garasanin, a minister in the Principality of Serbia, drafted the "Nacertanije", had come alive once again. According to this draft, which becomes actual whenever a war erupts in the Balkans, Greater Serbia should cover all the territories "where there is even one Serb alive, or there is his grave."[1] According to that, the envisioned territories of Greater Serbia should comprise Croatia (Dalmatia, Krajina, and Slavonia), Bosnia-Herzegovina, Macedonia, Kosovo and Montenegro, and some parts of the neighbouring countries, Albania, Greece, Bulgaria, Romania, and Hungary[2].

Slobodan Milosevic was also building his career. He came to power in 1987 when he became the leader of the League of Communists of Serbia and then rose to the presidency of Serbia in 1989. His leadership marked a tumultuous period in the Balkans, characterised by ethnic tensions and conflicts, particularly during the breakup of Yugoslavia in the 1990s. But at ten years old, I zipped around on my roller skates without a clue that Yugoslavia was on the brink of falling apart.

INDEPENDENCE DAY

I sat in the third row in my classroom at Jelenka Vockic. The school was lively on any other day, but on that day, it was eerily silent. April sunrays were hitting the classroom windows as if trying to escape the cold air outside, creating light in the darkened classroom. I had completed my work just as my brother walked in. I had no idea what he was doing there. I chuckled, thinking he must have missed arguing with me. I watched him intently as he handed my teacher a small piece of white paper. He did not seem thrilled to be there, nor did my teacher to see him. She took it, unfolded it slowly, and as she was reading it, Husein kept his gaze on the paper, and I kept mine on him, curious as to what was happening. My teacher seemed sad when she called out my name. "You are done for the day, Nadina," she said. I would later find out that my father had informed my teacher I was due for a hospital appointment. That was a lie.

I got up, placed my books in my red backpack, took my jacket, and as I walked toward the door, her hand patted me on the back. "See you tomorrow," she said. "See you," I responded.

Husein and I exited, walking side by side through the wide hallways, bright sunshine streaming through the tall windows as though everything was normal. Without saying a word, he looked at me in a way that I knew not to say anything.

We walked across the street, then over the train tracks that were now becoming hidden by grass. I had crossed these unused train tracks a thousand times going to school, so one more time made no difference. We continued to walk in silence, but my curiosity was killing me, and he could see that. He said, "We are going to Croatia for a week, but don't ask questions just yet." I remained silent but was also a bit excited about this sudden trip.

We stepped into our apartment, and all I could see was general chaos unfolding. Mama kept tucking her long fringe behind her ear, rushing around packing. Instead of her usual stylish skirt and blouse she always wore for work, she wore black trousers and a top. I followed her while she pulled clothes from various dresser drawers and stuffed them into a small piece of hand luggage. But her packing was not like packing for a vacation; it looked stressful and haphazard, with everything being done at breathtaking speed. I knew something was wrong. I knew then this was not a vacation. I knew we had to leave. I may have been a child, but I also had a pretty good idea that something was awry. I also knew that we were to become the same as those refugees from Vukovar whose bus stopped in our town. I knew that had we not left, we would have been killed or taken to a concentration camp to be tortured. I joined in, packing my Barbie and her clothes. Mama continued to pack. There was little talking, just taking items from one place and putting them in another. It seemed Mama was everywhere at once—the bedroom I shared with Husein, the dining room, my parents' bedroom, a staging area for packing everything our family would need for the week. One week. This is how long we all thought the war would last in the newly minted independent Republic of Bosnia and Herzegovina.

About six weeks before, on March 1, 1992, the referendum of independence saw a turnout of 63.4 percent of eligible voters, with an overwhelming 99.7 percent voting in favour of Bosnia and Herzegovina's independence. The declaration of independence marked the end of Bosnia's union with the Socialist Federal Republic of Yugoslavia (SFRJ), a federation that had been in place since the end of World War II. The move toward independence was part of a broader trend of disintegration within Yugoslavia, driven by rising ethnic nationalism and the collapse of communist regimes across Eastern Europe. The independence referendum was supported by Bosniaks (Bosnian Muslims) and Bosnian Croats, whereas it was largely boycotted by Bosnian Serbs. For Bosnian people, including my own family, recognising Bosnia as an independent republic meant independence from Serbia's dictatorship, and preventing it from stealing our resources to take to Serbia. It meant that Bosnian people could finally decide their own future and build their own life independent of the abusive Serbian regime. Yugoslavia opposed the democratic vote that led to independence and launched military actions to secure territory, conducted ethnic cleansing against Bosniaks and Croats, and took territory they ethnically cleansed as their own in order to create Greater Serbia where only Serbs lived.

But the independence did not come without its price. Some 40 kilometres from Brcko, the Yugoslav People's Army (JNA), which was the military branch of the SFRJ, surrounded Bijeljina. Serbian paramilitaries known as Arkan's Tigers began to butcher the town's Bosniak population. According to a top-secret CIA intelligence report, the Red Star Belgrade soccer team's fan club, known as the Delije, became a source of recruits for Arkan's Serbian Volunteer Guard in the early 1990s. According to US diplomatic reports, the fan club began offering paramilitary-style training to members in late 1990, including instruction in hand-to-hand combat, firearms use, and explosives. There were indications that the Red Star organisation had connections to Serbian police and security services at the time. The transformation of soccer hooligans into paramilitary fighters highlights how existing social structures were mobilised as Yugoslavia disintegrated into conflict.[3] They began to bomb the town, and murder, torture, and rape Bosniak civilians. American photojournalist Ron Haviv was there at the time and took photos that are the most significant evidence of genocide against Bosniak civilians. His photographs, especially the ones showing paramilitary troops executing civilians, became iconic images that drew global attention to the violence happening in Bosnia. This marked the beginning of the Bosnian War.

The Bijeljina massacre is considered one of the early acts of ethnic cleansing that defined much of the conflict in Bosnia, as Bosnian Serb forces aimed to create a Serb-dominated territory in Bosnia. The widespread media coverage of the Bijeljina massacre helped raise awareness about the escalating violence in Bosnia.

❖

Everyone in Brcko heard about what had happened, and fear was palpable. Bijeljina was just next door, and the once-cheerful town of Brcko on the Sava River now felt ominous and tense.

Soon after Bijeljina, the streets of Brcko were occupied by strange, bearded men speaking with a Serbian dialect and carrying holstered guns. They observed everyone. The situation was tense, and I was no longer allowed to go to the library on my own. Something was happening, but in a way, some people still didn't take it seriously. But on the day my brother turned up at my school, Mama had run into an old school friend who was now a detective. He seemed agitated and she asked him if he was alright. He told her that Serbs were stationed on all listening outposts, listening to everyone's phones, and that trouble was brewing. He told Mama that he and his wife were leaving in the evening and that we should go too. Mama hurried home to tell my father, but he was reluctant to leave, not believing that it was going to be that bad. This was the case with everyone in Bosnia. Everyone was in denial. But Mama stood her ground and told him she would take my brother and me and cross the bridge over the Sava into Croatia on foot that day if he didn't want to go. He realised that she was serious and went to get a car from his nephew.

We left almost everything behind. We carried just a small suitcase. We left everything we knew and that was part of us. All our belongings, including family photos. Even the lunch Mama had prepared for us that day. We left the apartment as if we were to return to it shortly.

We headed to my Aunt Rahima's place to pick up my cousin Tanja, who just an hour earlier, my father had told to pack and meet us in front of her building. Aunt Rahima didn't want to go. She, like many, was in denial. When we arrived in front of her building, she stood with Tanja as if she was sending her off for a weekend break. We chatted a little bit with my aunt, and she seemed as though she thought we were ridiculous for thinking some major war was going to erupt. When Tanja got into the car, Aunt Rahima waved us goodbye, smiling as if we were setting off on an adventure.

Our next stop was my maternal grandmother's house. She was home alone; my grandfather had passed away two years prior. She was home with her German Shepherd, Oskar. When we arrived, my father beeped the horn of the car, and she came out wearing her usual pants, shirt, and sweater and carrying a kitchen towel like she always did, an eternal cook always on her feet in the kitchen. Oskar saw the commotion and ran to the gate, but my grandma locked it behind her so that he stayed within the grounds of the house. A couple of years earlier he had jumped on Mama and me, so Mama wasn't a fan of his. One by one, we hugged my grandma. She, like my aunt, had no intention of leaving and thought we were exaggerating the threat. She hugged everyone, especially Mama, Husein, and me and said, "See you when you get back!"

We were on the road now. The sound of laughter rang throughout the car. It was as if we were going on one of our summer vacations. I perched between Tanja and Husein. I had a better view of the road from the middle, resting my elbows on the back of my parents' seats. On this smooth road, not a drop of snow was in sight. It looked like one of those midsummer evenings when it was still so light, and the sun's rays changed the sky's colour.

I suddenly remembered I had left my retainer in the bathroom of our Brcko apartment but did not know how to precisely deliver the news to my parents, who had often had to tell me off for not wearing it. I decided to get it over and done with, and said, "I left my retainer in the bathroom." Mama, looking at the road ahead, responded jokingly, "Maybe some Chetnik[4] will be wearing it from now on." The laughter continued. I thought, Phew, I'm out of the woods. But when I think back on Mama's response, it could have been some form of subconscious realisation she had that real trouble was hitting Brcko. That was maybe what she knew but would not admit to herself or us. But here we were on the road, supposedly to spend Easter in Croatia, although we did not celebrate Easter. I felt excited. I didn't fully comprehend what the situation was, but from previous events that I heard discussed between my parents, I was getting an idea.

Suddenly, five Serbian paramilitaries wearing dark khaki army-like uniforms jumped out of nowhere onto the main road and stopped our car by pointing guns and waving their hands indicating to us to stop. This was different from the border patrol. Instead, this was a makeshift checkpoint because the side road off the main road led to a cadet training centre, which is where they came from. Mama would later tell me that when she was in school, she had Defence and

Protection classes, and they would take them to that place to learn to shoot. But on that day, the barracks housed Serb paramilitaries. They were dirty, scruffy, and unshaven, as if they hadn't showered in days. They didn't look like an army.

The speed at which our laughter subsided was astonishing. My father stopped the car. One soldier knocked on the window with the muzzle of his gun, indicating with his hand to roll down the window. The Chetnik then peered in, looking at the back seat, then he looked at Mama and, in his Serbian dialect, asked, "Where are you going?" My father responded, "To visit our family in Croatia for Easter." But the soldier was not buying it. He ordered us out of the car. There was no politeness about it. He had the power, and he knew it.

Two paramilitary soldiers then began to search the inside of the car, front and back, while the other went through the boot. Then, finally, I could hear the loud thump as the car's boot shut. A soldier checking our documents told my father, "You are not the owner of this vehicle." My father responded, "It is my nephew's car. We sold ours and plan to buy a new one." Another soldier began to move down the line, pinning us against our car. I stood between my brother and cousin while the soldier went individually with his gun pointing at each person until it was pointed at me. The terror that gripped me was unlike anything I'd ever known—a primal, all-consuming fear that turned my blood to ice. My body betrayed me, trembling uncontrollably. My legs felt like jelly, threatening to buckle at any moment. The contrast between this moment of sheer horror and the normality of my life just hours before was staggering, leaving me disoriented and struggling to process what was happening. The fear was paralysing, rooting me to the spot. I could hear my heartbeat thundering in my ears, drowning out everything else. The memory of that soldier, that gun, that moment of terror... It haunts me still, a vivid reminder of how quickly life can change.

The carefree laughter of childhood feels like a distant echo, drowned out by the harsh reality of war. That checkpoint... God, that checkpoint. It stands like a grim milestone in my mind, marking the end of everything I knew and the beginning of a nightmare I couldn't wake up from.

What I witnessed there carved itself into my very being, leaving scars that run deeper than any physical wound. It's as if a part of me changed that day, replaced by a constant, gnawing fear and an understanding of cruelty that no child should ever have to bear. My childhood ended in that moment, crushed under the weight of war's brutal reality.

But that was what the soldiers wanted. They had the power and they knew it. They could've killed any of us that day. They weren't picky. "Where are you going?" he asked my parents again. Mama responded, "It's Easter in three days. We're going to Croatia to see our family. You can see we don't have much with us."

At that very moment, a white Golf sped past, and the Chetniks shot their guns in the air and shouted for the driver to stop. But the car did not stop. We heard one soldier say, "Go after him. If he doesn't stop, shoot at his tires." They returned our documents and told us we could go. The urgency with which we scrambled into our car was indescribable, and we drove away. I remember Mama continuously turning around to see if they would shoot at our car and kept making sure we were alright. But they did not. What happened to the occupant of the white Golf? I never knew, but it was like a miracle that appeared on that day to save us from whatever our fate would be. It is as though God saved us that afternoon at the makeshift checkpoint by sending that white Golf.

We continued our journey toward the Croatian border. The sun was setting, the weather was getting colder, and the snow on the roads had turned black from passing vehicles. We reached the border where the Croat border force acting alongside Croatian Defence Council (HVO) controlled the checkpoint. When we stopped, the HVO and border police checked the car. Right after seeing our registration, one of the members of the HVO asked, "Has it started there too?" Mama responded, "Not yet, but it looks like it will any day." Croats were at war with Serbia too, and this conversation took place while they checked our documents. After a few minutes, they let us pass. We had finally crossed into Croatia, another war zone, although not swallowed whole like Bosnia was about to be. We were now officially refugees. And although Croatia was also at war, its defences were much more robust as they were well-armed from weapons that arrived via their seaports, and there were areas free of war, such as Zagreb, its capital, which was well protected by a massive military police presence.

The roads were packed with other cars, all the headlights on full beam. It seemed like rush hour. Everyone was driving everywhere. Suddenly, we saw a vehicle with ZG (for Zagreb) registration plates flashing its headlights behind us. My parents questioned whether we should stop, but this was Croatia. It was different, even though there was no certainty.

Eventually, my father pulled up in a small resting space off the road, and the car pulled in behind us. As my father was exiting the vehicle, he told the rest of us to stay inside. The driver, in his mid-fifties, slim built, got out of his car and told my father he had seen our car registration and wanted to know if the war had started in Brcko too. Mama heard this and got out of the car. The man introduced himself to my parents as Mato and explained that his mother lived in a suburb of Brcko, and he wanted to know what the situation was, so he knew how to get her out. They spoke for a few minutes, and Mato told my parents that he knew people in Pula, a seafront city in Croatia where there were a lot of Bosnian refugees. He said it would be best to stay in Zagreb overnight because it was a long drive to Pula. He told us to follow him to a hotel in the city centre. We got into our car and did just that.

Mato, a Bosnian Croat, was a restaurant owner in Zagreb. He was also a genuinely kind man who did not have to help us but did. As the war spread around the former republics, the kindness of strangers would sometimes act as a buffer for a displaced person or a refugee. Not many people understood that, but Mato understood because his country was under attack too.

We arrived at the hotel. It was late and we were all tired, but my parents and Mato wanted to talk, so we ended up having dinner with him at the hotel. I remember the big round table and Mato sitting between my parents. Again, I was an audience to this conversation. Surprisingly, no one wanted to sleep. Mato was like a breath of fresh air. He knew people in Croatia and would help us more than he would know. The conversation centred on what had been happening in Croatia. It was like a rundown of the latest events in the most extended and detailed form. Eventually, we finished dinner. Just before Mato left, he told us he would come to see us early in the morning and bring information regarding Pula and where to go.

A SILENT GOODBYE

In the morning, sometime around six, we were awakened by a massive explosion that shook the hotel. I recognised the sound of those bombs because I had heard them before from our apartment in Brcko during the bombing across the Sava River. In the late evenings in Brcko, while the light was turned off in our apartment, I sometimes saw explosions in the distance in Gunja. But they did not have the same effect as the bomb exploding so close to the hotel. Sometime later, the rumour mill was ripe that Serbian intelligence had bombed a Jewish cultural centre. Some even said that Croats had bombed it to pin the blame on the Serbs. It did not matter who did it, it was done, and thankfully, no one was hurt. It had woken Mama, Tanja, and me. Even thirty minutes after that, it was still so dark. It seemed like the morning light would not break through the darkness anytime soon. Annoyed, I asked Mama when the sun would rise in Zagreb. My cousin and Mama joked, "Call reception and ask."

Eventually, the sun rose, as if it knew I was impatiently waiting for it. We got ready and headed downstairs to the restaurant where we were to meet Mato. He gave us clear instructions to head to a charity in Pula, where there were a lot of Bosnian refugees, as well as Croat refugees. He even gave us the names of the Croatian couple running the operation and said they were expecting us. He had called them and arranged everything for us. We promised to keep in touch with him. Mato shook hands with my parents, patted me on the head, and waved goodbye as he left. But when my father headed to the reception desk to check out and pay the bill, he was informed that Mato had paid all of it. My parents couldn't believe it and felt uncomfortable with that level of generosity. To say that was the kindness of strangers would not be correct; it was more than kindness, but Mato was no longer a stranger. He was now our friend. And even when my father called him to tell him he should not have paid and that he would like to return the money, Mato was unwilling to listen, saying we had helped him with information regarding Brcko. I would later learn that the information we gave him prompted him to go get his mother. With the help of HVO, Mato drove to Brcko and rescued his mother within days of meeting us.

Eventually, we were on the road again with extremely detailed directions to Pula because some towns in Croatia were engulfed in the war, so we had to avoid them. What should have been around a 300-kilometre drive was even longer. Everywhere was covered in snow. It was deadly cold and grey as if life had been sucked out of it, and in some places, life had been forcibly removed. The windows of houses by the road were smashed, and the houses themselves looked empty. Some roofs were burned. It was like driving through ghost towns. People had lived there once, but not anymore. There was so much emptiness. The only other vehicle we saw was a UN truck carrying peacekeepers. They looked at us as sadly as we did them. They were all young men sent to keep the peace but not get involved in a brutal conflict.

It was late afternoon, and the sun had already set when we got to the charity in Pula. There were so many people waiting to be processed. All were refugee women, children, and older people, Bosnians and Croats. They looked hungry and exhausted, waiting for shelter. But when we arrived, we headed straight into the office and asked for the people operating the charity. And after a few hours, they had an apartment for us with an old lady. We were to stay in a two-bedroom because there were five of us.

The apartment was in an old, cold building. It was so cold, as if no heat had ever touched the walls. That night would be as cold as if we had slept outside. Mama, Tanja, and I shared a double bed while my father and brother were in the other room. I don't know why that night was so cold, but it was below freezing, and we did not have enough blankets to warm ourselves. The comforts of the home we had left behind were like a distant memory. We were strangers in this frozen house. But nothing was worse than in the morning when Mama saw a mouse in the cold bathroom and went to my father to tell him there was no way we were staying in that house for another second. The house was freezing, and the mouse was a breaking point for Mama. We were used to a certain lifestyle, and though we were not expecting luxury, we did not expect the sixth occupant to be a mouse.

We were on the move again after we thanked the old lady for letting us stay the night. We were headed back to Zagreb, to the same hotel where an amused Mato was expecting us. This time, it was a little less dramatic. No religious organisations were being bombed. Mato told us of a spa in Krapinske Toplice housing Croatian Defence Forces (HOS) and their families. HOS was under the leadership of a Croat politician, Dobroslav Paraga. He had briefly been in the same party as Croatia's President Franjo Tudjman but left to form his own Croatian Party of Rights. HOS had the same aim as the Bosnian army: to fight against the Serbs. We arrived in Krapinske Toplice on April 20.

The spa was almost on the front line, and depending on how heavy the fighting was, the HOS was either in the resort resting or running with guns to the front line. But the spa was secure, and there was no fear that we would be attacked. I developed friendships with the children of HOS members, so there were no dull days. It also gave us kids a chance to forget that there was a war. We used the swimming pool every chance we got. And in the evening when our parents held conversations with other refugees there, sometimes we sat and listened. The talk was always about the war. No one talked about happier times anymore. It's as if they had forgotten them. I was spending a lot more time with my parents, with Husein and Tanja. And when my parents travelled to Zagreb, Tanja was the babysitter, a job she didn't take seriously because she joined in the fun with all of us. But we were limited in what we could do. That was, after all, a wartime situation. I did not attend school during this time, even though the school year had not ended. But it was here that we found out we would never return to Brcko.

On April 30, 1992, fourteen days after becoming refugees, while sitting in the entertainment room with other families and some HOS soldiers watching TV, news broke from Brcko of a major massacre. Over one hundred Bosniaks and Bosnian Croats had tried to cross the bridge in the early morning to head to Gunja in Croatia, but the bridge was deliberately blown up, killing everyone. Body parts flew across the town, some landing through people's windows and in their gardens, others into the Sava River. It became known as the Brcko Bridge massacre, yet no one faced justice. It was believed that White Eagles and Arkan's Tigers were responsible. The White Eagles were a Serbian paramilitary group associated with the Serbian Radical Party. Both fought in Croatia and Bosnia, committing war crimes. The news showed the moments the bridge was blown up and the carnage that followed. Upon seeing this, Mama began to cry and ran out of the room. I, Tanja, and some wives of HOS soldiers ran after her. She was crying because not only was this confirmation that Brcko was under attack and that we would never return, but also our family—Grandma Sadika, Aunt Rahima, Uncle Huso—were still there and would be hunted.

Born and raised in the labyrinthine streets of Brcko, Mama had a deep connection with the city that started with her birth mother, Mara.

Mara moved to Brcko to study economics, partly because her brother was the military commander there. During her studies, she fell in love with a classmate, but their happiness was overshadowed by the difficulties of impending parenthood and strong opposition from their families. In post–World War II Yugoslavia, despite many inter-ethnic and inter-religious marriages, neither family accepted their relationship.

Mara was the daughter of a Serb, and the man she'd fallen in love with was a Bosnian Croat. Their relationship was controversial because Serbs and Croats had a history of animosity, partly due to the atrocities committed in Jasenovac, a notorious concentration camp operated by Croatia's Ustase regime during World War II. Jasenovac was infamous for the large number of Jews, Roma, and Serbs who were murdered there. Despite the hostility, Mara and her Bosnian Croat boyfriend believed in their love, and they were excited to have a child together.

By 1959, when Tito had been in power for a decade and a half, and Yugoslavia had shifted from communism to socialism, Mara gave birth to a daughter. The country was experiencing prosperity and had witnessed record harvests. The Great War seemed like a distant memory, and there was hope for a better future. Mara and her partner saw Western culture starting to influence their lives and looked forward to improvements in living conditions, healthcare, and education.

In the summer of 1959, Mara stood on a bridge between Gunja and Brcko, contemplating whether to keep her child or give her up. Her confusion stemmed from the pressure exerted by her brother and the rest of the family, given that the baby's father was Bosnian Croat and not a Serb. As she struggled with this decision, a Bosniak man intervened and helped her. This Bosniak man and his wife ended up adopting Mara's daughter. This adoption, a Serbian child being raised by Bosniaks, highlighted the resilience of the human spirit in the face of historical challenges.

Mama grew up in Brcko, a city that would eventually become a refuge amidst the war. When she was about ten or eleven, she met Mara, who was introduced as an aunt from France. Even then, Mama, who had a keen interest in history and literature, sensed that Mara was her biological mother saying a silent goodbye.

Mama found comfort in the river Sava, becoming an excellent swimmer and navigating its waters with skill. The river, once a symbol of danger, became her sanctuary and a testament to her resilience. Her strength, developed through her challenging youth, remains a testament to her enduring spirit.

BROKEN

After spending a month in Krapinske Toplice, we moved to Zagreb, settling into a house farther from the city centre. A Bosnian imam with his wife and two daughters lived on the ground floor of the house opposite. One of the daughters was close to my age. The family hailed from Tuzla, roughly fifty kilometres from Brcko. Conversations between my father and the imam often revolved around the situation in Bosnia, with the imam sharing valuable insights. Meanwhile, Mama and the imam's wife would sometimes drink coffee together, alternating between our homes, while I bonded with their children. The imam's calm demeanour and kindness left a lasting impression on me, shaping my expectations of others in similar roles. In the loud chaos of the war, the calmness of people like him prevailed.

During this time, my father, working as a translator with UNPROFOR, frequently travelled across Croatia with military higher-ups, leaving home for long stretches. But we were always safe in Zagreb. However, an incident while playing in the courtyard with my brother left me with an injured ankle, the severity only becoming apparent upon a visit to the hospital. The journey there, marked by the care of the tram driver and the concern of passersby, emphasised the community's solidarity.

The hospital, nestled amidst lush greenery, initially resembled a sanctuary rather than a medical facility. However, the sight of injured soldiers, their agony palpable, quickly shifted the atmosphere. Despite the chaos, the medical staff, notably a friendly Croat doctor, provided compassionate care. Amidst discussions about music and moments of levity, I found solace from the war's horrors. Perhaps I offered a reprieve for the doctor as well, who told me that I was a break from the horrors of the war-wounded moaning in agony in the waiting room.

Grateful for the kindness, we bid farewell to the hospital staff as though parting ways with old friends. Even during war, acts of compassion from strangers remained abundant.

Life continued in Zagreb, and my father's work with the peacekeepers marked the onset of various generals affiliated with UNPROFOR visiting our home to confer with my father. Among them, the most memorable was a distinguished member of the Jordanian army, who arrived clad in military attire in a military vehicle accompanied by a driver, bearing gifts for my brother and me. He presented my brother with a sabre sword–like pin and gave me a black elephant figurine, which instantly became my most cherished possession. Seeing my broken foot in plaster, the general jokingly enquired whether I too had been at the front line of the war.

Seated across from my father and the general, I was captivated by the intricate details of the general's uniform, observing how it accentuated his commanding presence. Despite the gravity of his responsibilities, he exuded warmth and gave occasional smiles, particularly when war-related topics were set aside. Engaging in conversations fuelled by my father's insights, the general displayed a keen interest in subjects beyond the battlefield.

During his visit, the general shared alarming updates about Bosnia's plight, highlighting the urgency for intervention, especially from the Arab world. King Fahd of Saudi Arabia emerged as a key supporter of the Bosnian people during our time of crisis. Unlike Western leaders, his dedication was unwavering, as noted by President Bill Clinton who said King Fahd was the only figure persistently advocating for international intervention in Bosnia, despite its lack of strategic importance.[5] King Fahd donated $8 million personally and founded the Saudi High Commission for Relief of Bosnia, led by his brother, now King Salman bin Abdulaziz Al Saud. This commission donated further millions of dollars' worth of aid. This organisation became a crucial lifeline for the Bosnian people. King Fahd's support extended beyond financial aid; he urged Muslims worldwide to stand with Bosnia and made direct appeals to global leaders, including the US president.[6] His humanitarian efforts not only provided essential assistance but also raised international awareness, helping shape Bosnia's struggle for survival and possibly saving countless lives.

When the general departed, his parting words of encouragement lingered, a reminder of the interconnectedness despite turmoil. Though his visit was brief, its impact resonated deeply, underscoring the importance of solidarity amidst adversity.

Horrors were unfolding back home in Bosnia, in marked contrast to life in Zagreb, which was monotonous in a comforting way. I believe it was our neighbour imam who introduced my father to Dr Mustafa Ceric, who would soon become the Grand Mufti of Bosnia and Herzegovina. Occasionally, there would be some documents to translate, so my father did that for him. That provided extra income and connections that would later prove valuable. Zagreb was swarming with Bosnians but Croat refugees too. International organisations were everywhere, as was the Croatian military police. Bosnians from public life visited often. Stories of rape and torture began to emerge from across the country. The stories would consume the meetups my parents regularly attended. Those meetups were the only way to know what was going on. There was no social media back then. The meetups were often held at Trg Bana Jelacica, the grand square in Zagreb bustling with bars, restaurants, chocolate shops, and patisseries. The fountain provided much-needed entertainment, and our favourite pizza restaurant was nearby. You could get there by tram, but Mama and I preferred to walk as much as we could. We'd join so many refugees assembled in the square, some from our hometown. I would socialise with my peers and my parents with theirs.

On one of our walks, we met the famous Bosnian Sevdah singer, Safet Isovic, whose music was always heard in our house, even to this day. When Mama greeted him, he looked at her and instantly smiled upon hearing a Bosnian accent. He was in Zagreb for treatment after sustaining an injury when his Sarajevo apartment was bombed. They chatted, and he called her *moja Bosanka* (my Bosnian). When we parted,

Isovic pulled her in for a hug and a peck on the cheek. It was a little bit of Bosnian soul on that street during the war on that sunny Zagreb day.

But when we headed to the Stone Gate, a landmark in the Upper Town of Zagreb, a historic location that required some energy to reach via cobbled streets and a hill, we would light the candles just below the Stone Gate for the souls of our relatives who had passed away. There were always so many women, young and old, lighting candles for their loved ones. I often wondered how many of those women lighting candles found solace, at least for a moment. But this candle lighting became a tradition for Mama and me, and we went there often. This was not a religious thing, it was a form of spirituality, and something Mama and Aunt Rahima used to do together regularly in Brcko, so Mama and I kept the tradition in Zagreb. I am sure if Aunt Rahima was there, she would have loved lighting candles with us too.

By August 1992, the international media began to report on rape camps run by Serbian soldiers where Bosniak women were raped along with very young girls. The first to break that story was Newsday's American correspondent Roy Gutman who later received a Pulitzer Prize for his reporting on the Bosnian War. At this point I was more aware and in tune with the war than I needed to be at that age. I now fully understood what was going on and what crimes were being committed. This heightened awareness became my new normal, as if I had matured in the span of a single night. I was no longer a carefree child from Brcko, but rather a fully cognisant individual grappling with harsh realities. It was like my brain was working like a grown-up, even though I was still a kid. The war changed how I saw everything, and I couldn't un-see it.

The reports coming from Bosnia were about women who were raped repeatedly to humiliate them, sometimes in front of other women. Guards would take turns. Some women were killed after being raped multiple times. Some managed to escape and get to Zagreb. Dr Ceric had been informed of all that was taking place and had been told that Britain was unwilling to lift a finger to help the Bosnian people. So, he asked my father to take surviving raped Bosniak women to London to get their message to the British government. The trip would be funded by the Bosnian administration and the Bosnian Islamic community and organised by Dr Ceric. My father agreed. He had been an English language professor in Brcko, so he was fluent in the language, and he and Mama were already campaigning to end the war in Bosnia, so he was the natural choice for the mission.

It was late August when he arrived in London, where he would soon find that the British Conservative government couldn't care less whether people were tortured in concentration camps or that women and girls were being raped. Moreover, the British government refused to vote to lift the arms embargo so the Bosnian Army could defend us.[7]

While in London, my father met with people like Professor Noel Malcolm, and journalists Ed Vulliamy and Maggie O'Kane, who were following or reporting on the war from the start. They were enraged by what was being allowed to happen in Bosnia. My father met some British Croats who were staunch supporters of the Bosnian people, and an English lawyer, Jerry, who was working on bringing humanitarian aid to Bosnia. The British people were angry with their government, but the government ignored them.

My father's trip was unsuccessful in helping those raped women. But the new people he met would help us, including a Croat professor who, during an event, asked my father if he'd like to be more centrally located near good schools for my brother and me. She told him her mother had an apartment for rent in Kvaternikov Trg, which could be ours for a fair price. Soon after my father's return to Zagreb, we moved in.

GRANDMA'S SONG

In September 1992, our family faced its first loss. I still vividly remember the sombre atmosphere on that rainy day in Zagreb when we received the news. Mama sat in silence, clutching the phone tightly while she spoke with Nisa, Grandma's sister. This heartbreaking event occurred shortly after we moved to our apartment in Kvaternikov Trg.

Nisa must have relayed the news quickly, because Mama soon fell into a heavy silence that matched the damp atmosphere outside, where trees swayed under the weight of each gust of rain. I watched the colour drain from Mama's face as she clutched the heavy receiver to her ear. When Mama's sobs shattered the oppressive stillness, it became clear to me that Grandma Sadika, Mama's mother, had passed. She died in a refugee camp in Czechoslovakia at the age of sixty-seven. Mama's grief poured out in the hours and days that followed.

At that moment, our family was scattered. Tanja, still with us in Zagreb, was preparing to leave for Berlin that very day with an old friend from Brcko who was also heading to Germany. She felt she could build a better life there, especially since some of her friends were already living as refugees in Berlin. Meanwhile, her mother, Aunt Rahima, remained in

Brcko. Like countless others in Bosnia, they initially believed that the war wouldn't reach them, and that even if it did, it would be brief. They held on to the hope of being spared, convinced that the international community would step in before any harm could come to them.

I wished Grandma had been with us in Croatia. I know she would have loved it. I could picture her in our kitchen, cooking all day with a kitchen towel always within reach. I know that if Aunt Rahima was with us too, she would have been out with Mama and me. Yet, Aunt Rahima was among the 3,500 men, women, and children, mostly Bosniaks, who were tortured and forcibly detained in the Luka concentration camp in Brcko. These were people who lived either in Brcko itself or the suburbs.

Although some might consider Aunt Rahima fortunate not to have perished alongside the thousands of men, women, and children who were tortured, killed, and incinerated in the city's kafilerija factories, her ordeal was nonetheless harrowing. Held in that dreadful place, she endured the horrors of multiple rapes by numerous Serbian soldiers. I learned later that Aunt Rahima remained in the concentration camp until it closed in July 1992. Upon her release, she was confined to her own apartment, where she suffered further assaults. Despite the agony, she somehow persuaded her captors to allow her to visit our apartment and gather a few mementos of our family. There, among scattered photos on the floor, she found a few scant reminders of our family's past. Shortly after my aunt's visit, our apartment was occupied by a family from Serbia.

Uncle Huso shared the same fate and was detained in the Luka camp. Enduring the same inhumane treatment and torture inflicted upon others, he emerged from captivity with both physical and mental scars.

But on that September day in Zagreb, my parents united in their efforts to begin the process of transferring Grandma Sadika's remains from the refugee camp in Gabcikovo, Slovakia, formerly Czechoslovakia, to Gunja in Croatia. Repatriating my grandmother's body to Brcko, where Serb forces maintained control, was too risky at that time.

As I sat beside Mama, a wave of emotion washed over me. I couldn't help but ponder whether Grandma Sadika was aware that this would be her final journey. She was the last grandparent I had, and the thought of losing her filled me with a bittersweet ache. In my childhood dreams, I had always wished for her to be with us for many more years, sharing stories and laughter.

Now, as I thought of her in that refugee camp, I couldn't shake the feeling of longing for the warmth and comfort of her home. What must have been going through her mind as she sat there, surrounded by uncertainty? Did she reminisce about the life she once knew? My heart ached for her, for the sacrifices she made, and for the love that still bound us together, even in the most challenging of circumstances.

Once Mama reached out to the Czechoslovakian embassy in Zagreb, the Czech authorities responded swiftly and efficiently. I listened intently while she spoke on the phone, her words clear and precise. Looking back, I realise she was likely still in shock, focusing on the tasks at hand and methodically ticking them off one by one. Mama was doing what needed to be done, moving forward in the same meticulous manner she always had, even in the face of grief.

Through experience, I've come to understand that grief manifests in myriad ways.

Before long, Grandma Sadika's remains crossed the Croatian border in a sealed wooden casket. My father stood waiting at the border with two representatives from a Croatian funeral service company, arranged by my parents. Upon crossing into Croatia, my grandmother's body was placed under their care, and together with my father, they proceeded to Gunja. As for my father's emotions in that moment, it's difficult to say for certain, except for a deep sense of duty to ensure his mother-in-law received dignified treatment in death. Perhaps he harboured a hope that this act could, in some small measure, ease the immense loss our family had suffered. The details of her final months and days in that camp remain elusive, much like the suffering she likely endured when torn from the cherished home she held dear.

WAR CHILD

In Zagreb, the war seemed a distant echo. I walked alone to my new school through the bustling streets of Croatia's capital. Childhood felt like a faded dream, a memory from another life. War casts its shadow, where right and wrong entwine, friend and foe blur, and borders melt into uncertainty. Just months before, in Brcko, I had been a child in a serene Bosnian port town, my days filled with joy and the comfort of safety.

As I roamed freely in Zagreb, my thoughts often drifted to my peers enduring the horrors of the Sarajevo siege, which started just before our departure from Bosnia. While I strolled peacefully to school in Zagreb, across the border in Sarajevo, the hills and mountains occupied by General Ratko Mladic's Serbian army echoed with the deadly crackle of sniper fire, indiscriminately targeting anyone in motion, tragically including innocent children. While I casually visited bakeries in Zagreb, in Sarajevo, lines formed as people waited desperately for a loaf of bread or to fill their canisters with water. While Zagreb teemed with sufficient food, Sarajevo faced days of starvation. While the night sky above Zagreb sparkled serenely with stars, in Sarajevo, it was pierced by the relentless barrage of shelling and bombing, engulfing the city in a fiery inferno, leaving behind a trail of destruction, consuming homes, schools, markets, and every semblance of normality.

I was constantly listening to conversations about war. It became the most normal conversation to hear my parents have, as if there was nothing else to talk about, but it was not surprising, because at that time what else was there to talk about? It's as if I was an observer of the war, watching like the UN peacekeepers but doing nothing. If there ever was a time to learn about the politics of the war, that was it.

Looking back, the shift from childhood to adulthood felt so sudden. There was no gradual transition; there was only "before the war" and "after the war." Before, my brother and I squabbled over trivial matters, like who got the control of the TV remote. Then suddenly, we were fleeing for our lives.

At school, I was the solitary Bosniak among a sea of Croat faces. The air crackled with tension, thick with unspoken accusations and simmering resentments. Each day, I walked a tightrope of identity, balancing precariously between who I was and who I needed to be to survive.

The fathers of my classmates wore their patriotism like armour, returning from the front lines with tales of valour that set young hearts ablaze with nationalistic fervour. Their stories echoed through the hallways, a constant reminder of the divide that yawned between us.

Here, in this microcosm of a fractured nation, I witnessed firsthand how quickly the bonds of community could unravel, how swiftly neighbours could become nemeses. The lesson was as painful as it was profound: In times of war, the boundaries of friendship and enmity are as fluid as the front lines themselves, shifting with each passing day, redrawing the map of our lives with cruel indifference.

I had only one friend in that school. Her name was Katarina, and her father was a member of the HVO fighting against the Serbs. Despite the changing political landscape, she was still my friend. But there had been warning signs that tensions would rise between Croats and Bosniaks. It was inevitable. Although Croats and Serbs hated each other, their leaders Tudjman and Milosevic only saw eye to eye when it came to partitioning Bosnia, and all the conversations in our living room pointed to that. I couldn't grasp the concept of discrimination because, in Brcko, people of different religions and ethnicities coexisted as equals. Yet in Croatia I had my first introduction to discrimination. Here, the Croat kids didn't see me as their equal. They must have overheard their parents speaking negatively about Bosniaks and started echoing those sentiments. I became a third-class citizen at school, treated as a burden on the education system rather than a fellow human being. They hated me despite my innocence. Children are not born with hatred; it is instilled in them by their parents.

As I clung to the last vestiges of my childhood, the war's tendrils still snaked their way into the most sacred corners of my life, tainting even my friendship with Katarina. We were two sides of the same coin, our bond forged in the crucible of shared experiences and mirrored appearances. Our tall, slender frames and long dark hair, often bound in identical ponytails, made us seem like sisters separated at birth.

Each day, Katarina's presence in class was a balm to my soul, a shield against the barbs of bullies and the poisonous whispers that increasingly followed me. With her as my friend, I could almost believe in the illusion of normality, of belonging.

As I walked to school each morning, the familiar sights and sounds of the city wrapped around me like a comforting blanket. The bustling farmers' market, the aromatic restaurants, and the cozy cafes painted a picture of cosmopolitan life untouched by the brutality raging beyond our borders.

The small bakery became my daily refuge, a place where I could pretend that the world hadn't changed. The old lady behind the counter, her white coat crisp and clean, her hair neatly tucked away, became a symbol of constancy in a world spinning out of control. Her warm smile and twinkling eyes seemed to promise that some things would remain forever unchanged, a beacon of hope in the gathering storm.

In those fleeting moments, I could almost forget about the war. But deep down, I knew that this fragile peace was as delicate as spun sugar, ready to shatter at the slightest touch of reality.

And then, one day began as always with the comforting ritual at the bakery. The warm, sweet aroma of fresh pastries enveloped me as the kind-eyed lady handed me my white paper bag. The poppy-seed swirl, still warm, was a small joy I savoured, unaware that it would soon become a bittersweet memory.

When I arrived at school, Katarina's absence was a void that echoed through the classroom. Days stretched into a week, each one amplifying my concern. When she finally returned, the change in her was profound and heartbreaking.

The vibrant girl I knew had vanished, replaced by a shell of her former self. Her eyes, once bright with laughter, now held a darkness that seemed bottomless.

Learning of her father's death at the hands of a Serbian sniper was a blow that left us all reeling. Katarina's grief manifested in the bullet casing she wore around her neck—a stark, brutal reminder of her loss. Though I couldn't fathom carrying such a painful token, I recognised it as her way of keeping her father close, of honouring his memory in the only way she knew how.

Our friendship endured, but it was transformed. Katarina's silence spoke volumes, and I tried my best to be a comforting presence, even when words failed us both. The weight of her sorrow was palpable, and I often felt helpless in the face of such profound loss.

Sharing Katarina's story with Mama brought a new dimension to our understanding. Mama's empathy, born from her own experiences of war and loss, helped me navigate the complex emotions surrounding my friend's tragedy. Our conversations about Katarina became a way for us to process the senseless violence that had touched our lives.

When Katarina left for Austria with her mother, it felt like another casualty of the war. The sniper's bullet had not only taken her father but had also shattered her world, forcing her to leave behind everything familiar in search of a new beginning. Her departure left a void in my life, a stark reminder of how war ruthlessly reshapes destinies.

The war had not only changed the landscape of our country but was also scattering its people to the winds. Most of the people I knew had moved somewhere else.

JOURNEY OF A THOUSAND MILES

The war in Bosnia continued to rage, escalating the tension between Bosnia and Croatia. This was most evident to me at school, where the bullying became increasingly brutal. I remember one occasion when they wouldn't let me use the toilet, saying the toilets were only for Croatian kids and that Bosnians had to go outside. I had to wait for classes to start for all the kids to disperse, making myself late for class. This is what hate felt like. Croats had become monstrous, as evidenced by the actions of Tudjman and Milosevic tearing Bosnia apart.

A year since I became a refugee, on April 16, 1993, Croatia's HVO units committed a brutal massacre in the town of Ahmici, Bosnia and Herzegovina, claiming the lives of 116 Bosniaks, including a three-month-old baby. The atrocity unfolded in a horrific manner, with most of the men subjected to point-blank shooting by HVO forces. Croatian soldiers rounded up and executed several men, while around twenty individuals lost their lives attempting to escape across the fields, victims of marksmen's bullets.

The aftermath revealed further horrors, when charred remains in houses indicated some victims had been burned alive, rendering them unidentifiable. Among the tragic casualties were thirty-two women and eleven children. Prior to the onslaught, Bosnian Croat civilians had been evacuated from Ahmici, a chilling indicator of premeditation. Colonel Bob Stewart, who served as the UN Commander of British Forces, encountered the aftermath of this massacre. He later recounted the brutality in front of the British Parliament, describing how he walked into a cellar and found burnt bodies. He recalled a soldier turning to him and saying, "Sir, this is Europe in 1993, not Europe in 1943."

The news of the massacre and other information my father received from UNPROFOR indicated that the war in Bosnia was far from over. By this point, Jerry, the English lawyer and supporter of Bosnia my father had met in London was concerned and suggested to my parents to apply for a visa to move to the UK. My parents knew we had to leave. There was no choice, not with the war still raging and no end in sight. They were united in their determination to give us a better life, working together with a fierce, unwavering commitment. But even as they planned our escape, they never lost their deep love for Bosnia. It was as if they carried the weight of two worlds: the hope for our future and the enduring loyalty to the home they were being forced to leave. During those years, survival was paramount, and many Bosnians were fleeing to Austria and Germany, as both countries were still accepting refugees. At the British Consulate in Zagreb, my parents submitted a request to move to the UK.

Around this time my parents spoke about the former UK Prime Minister, Baroness Margaret Thatcher. Newspapers in Britain and America reported her passionate calls for military intervention to end the bloodshed in Bosnia. Her unwavering belief in Bosnia's multi-ethnic identity resonated deeply. She denounced the massacre as a stain on the West's conscience, rejecting the "civil war"[8] label often used by Western governments to shirk responsibility.

Thatcher's boldness drew criticism from John Major's Conservative government and the Defence Secretary, who dismissed her stance as "emotional nonsense."[9] The US Secretary of State Warren Christopher, largely unsupportive of Bosnia during the conflict, also derided her position.[10] But Thatcher's advocacy was not driven by mere emotion but by a steadfast commitment to ending the violence against Bosnian civilians, making her one of the lone voices among Western leaders in a country we were about to move to.

Before the war, my father had a deep affection for England, a place he had come to love while studying there as an exchange student. Even as an adult, he stayed connected to that world, subscribing to British political magazines that arrived in the post. I can still picture the plastic-wrapped tubes they came in, a small but constant reminder of a distant place. I used to flip through the pages, intrigued by the characters in the English language books, imagining their lives and the world they lived in. I expected England to be just like that, filled with people with names like Jane, Tom, and John—a place so different from Bosnia or Croatia.

The thought of moving to another country thrilled me, a mix of excitement and relief. It wasn't just the adventure of it, it was the hope of escaping the constant torment I faced at school in Zagreb, especially after Katarina left. The bullying had become unbearable, and the idea of leaving it behind filled me with a sense of hope I hadn't felt in a long time. My brother and I both longed for something stable, something normal—something that seemed impossible in Croatia. England felt like a promise of a better life, a place where we could finally find some peace and calm.

The days leading up to our eventual departure were tense. Bullying at school got worse, and more and more military police were on the streets. There were even times when Croatian military police arrested Bosnian males they deemed were of military age, even if they were not.

Within a week, the British Consulate in Zagreb notified my parents that we had been granted a family visa to move to the UK. Excitement filled me at the thought of going somewhere completely new, where the long shadow of the war couldn't reach me or my family. I hoped the schools there would not tolerate the bullying I had experienced in Zagreb.

We informed Jerry, who days later drove to Zagreb at the end of April. Jerry was a lanky old Englishman with curly blond hair. He ran his own corporate law firm in Northampton and was the founder of a charity, the Bosnian Support Group. A divorcé and an English eccentric, Jerry was constantly on the move, like a yo-yo. He loved the Bosnian food Mama cooked and always joined us for lunch or dinner whenever he visited. I remember his voice clearly; if there was ever a prime example of a posh English accent, his was it. And on many occasions when he came to our home, I would listen as he spoke, watching his mannerisms and how he pronounced words. Now that I knew I was moving to the UK, I thought this was a lesson in elocution. Of course, I don't have a posh accent, but it was fun copying his pronunciation, especially the way Jerry answered the phone, "Hell-oo" the long "o" at the end. I sometimes still copy that, like a small tribute to Jerry.

On May 1, 1993, Mama, Husein, and I settled into the back seat of Jerry's Ford, while my father and Jerry took the front. The two of them took turns driving on our nearly two thousand-kilometre journey that began in the middle of the night. When we left Brcko it had been rushed and dangerous; this instead was calmer and with a clear destination. Sitting in the back of the car for long hours was uncomfortable, but it was our only option. Every time we stopped for a break, I could barely stand up straight to stretch my legs, which felt locked in place from sitting for so long. We passed through many major European countries, a journey one might relish as an adult. I still remember the smoothness of the German motorways and the greenery in almost every country we passed through. In some places, the weather was warm; in others, it was cloudy, as if we were driving through changing seasons. I don't recall being stopped once. We were moving farther and farther away from Bosnia, closer and closer to England.

I didn't feel any sadness. Even at twelve years old, I understood that the situation in Croatia was dangerously unstable for Bosnians. If we were ever to stop being refugees, we had to seek stability elsewhere. I think, deep down, I saw England as a new beginning, a place full of possibilities. I had my own ideas and expectations, shaped by the stories I had heard.

After my father returned from a trip to London, he was disillusioned by Britain's politics, but even he believed it couldn't stay that way forever. Mama felt the same, though her focus was on escaping the relentless uncertainty and constant threats that engulfed Bosnia and Croatia. More than anything, she longed for a stable family life. She knew we could never return to the way things had been in Bosnia, but she was wise enough to understand that we had to move forward with the times.

My brother and I were eager to get to England, excited by the thought of a new adventure. But as we sat in the back seat, exhausted, we were like two weary travellers, caught between the past and the future, desperately hoping that this journey would finally bring us some peace.

It must have been on day two of this drive when we finally arrived in Calais and boarded a ferry to cross to Dover. Surprisingly, the ferry ride was peaceful, probably the only time it ever was.

In Dover, we encountered passport control. It was late at night, and the only illumination came from the bright ceiling lamps above the passport checking desk. Several uniformed officers were inspecting our documents in this cold, empty, and spacious area. We were the only ones there. Dover was typically a hotspot for catching illegal immigrants, but our process went smoothly because we had visas. After about thirty minutes, we were back in the car. We had entered the UK and were headed to Northampton, another three hundred or so kilometres away.

That night, as I leaned my head against the car window, the green fields in Britain took on a serene and mystical quality. Under the moonlight, the lush grass appeared silvered, casting a soft glow across the landscape. The fields may have been enveloped in a gentle mist—after all, the weather was ripe for it—adding to the ethereal atmosphere. Ancient hedgerows and dry-stone walls created dark, silhouetted lines against the faintly lit backdrop. Stars peppered the sky above, their light reflected faintly off the dewy grass. The occasional farmhouse or distant village emitted a warm, golden light, creating a comforting contrast to the cool, silvery tones of the fields. The night air was crisp and fresh, carrying the subtle scents of earth and foliage. I bet if I had walked through these fields at night like Miss Elizabeth Bennett in *Pride and Prejudice*, I would have felt a profound sense of peace and a deep connection to the timeless beauty of the British countryside, leaving my war behind.

PART II (1993–1998)

DROWNING THE SOUND

The morning of our arrival in Northampton, it was brilliantly sunny, as if the heavens were smiling upon us, welcoming us to safety. We felt refreshed despite arriving in the middle of the night. The atmosphere enveloped me in a sense of comfort and safety. As I looked at the charming Victorian houses scattered across the landscape, a profound feeling of calm washed over me.

That morning, Mama asked Jerry to drive her to a local college so she could enrol in English language classes. Jerry was taken aback by her request, exclaiming, "No one has ever taken the initiative to begin learning the language on their first day here. No one has ever asked me that question before." Mama's desire to enrol immediately in English classes came from a strong determination to integrate and adapt to our new life in the UK. She had a sense of hope and optimism to build a new life in Britain.

Despite his surprise, Jerry took Mama to the local college and assisted her with the enrolment process. Though she spoke little English, the college, nearing the end of the term, invited her to join a day trip to Cambridge with other students. She accepted the invitation but found communication challenging. Nonetheless, the trip was an excellent opportunity for her to practice speaking English and begin to move forward after a year of uncertainty.

Jerry was so welcoming that he insisted we stay in his house until we could find a place of our own. But to have our own house could only be done with the Home Office giving us full refugee status. So, a lawyer Jerry knew who dealt with immigration represented us. He quickly secured refugee status for us. That meant that our old Yugoslav passport had to be submitted to the Home Office, as it was no longer valid. We no longer had any passport, only a refugee status that didn't allow my parents to work, but at least my brother and I were enrolled in school and all of us had access to doctors and dentists and other services. The lawyer had made all other registrations on our behalf.

Our first days in Northampton were exciting. The town's historic architecture, including its medieval churches and centuries-old buildings, stood as testaments to Northampton's past. The cobblestone streets in the town centre, quiet and peaceful, evoked a sense of timelessness.

The town boasted a bustling farmers' market and a department store in its city centre. At the market, you could find anything you desired; there was no rationing akin to that in Zagreb during the war. Mama and I visited it frequently to buy organic fruits and vegetables needed to cook Bosnian dishes, whereas my brother, a teenager, preferred staying home, engrossed in his computer with his new friends with a shared interest. He was never one for walks and we couldn't make him do it; his gaze was always fixed on the computer screen.

And while Mama and I freely walked the streets of this peaceful city, a thousand of miles away the siege of Sarajevo was unfolding in the full glare of the international media. Just over two months after our arrival in the UK, in just one day, 3,777 shells fell on Sarajevo, shot from the surrounding hills occupied by the Serbian aggressor. The siege was a brutal component of the Bosnian Serb forces' broader campaign, led by Radovan Karadzic and General Mladic, aiming to ethnically cleanse and seize control of Bosniak territories.

I felt fortunate to be safe in England. The only thing I took shelter from was the British rain; they, on the other hand, sought shelter from raining shells and sniper bullets.

We gradually settled in this town, tucked away in safety and peace. The English people were incredibly hospitable. I remember a time when our TV stopped working. A neighbour a few houses down, who lived alone and had two TVs, generously gave us one, insisting we use it until we could get our own. Across from us lived a cheerful, elderly English couple who were exceptionally friendly. They offered us invaluable advice on navigating life in Britain. Their knowledge was extensive. The people of Northampton were warm and welcoming, embodying the kindness that characterised English people as a whole.

Their kindness continued to shine through when the school year commenced, and both my brother and I were enrolled in Trinity School. Every day, Husein and I walked together to and from school. The first day was a real nail-biter, mostly because, well, we were diving headfirst into a new language. Speaking English at home and mangling a few sentences was one thing, but this was a whole new ball game. School, where we had to survive in English all day long! But I think the nerves only lasted that first day for both me and my brother. We were mostly anxious about how we'd be welcomed, and whether the kids would be friendly or unleash their inner bullies, something I knew all too well from Zagreb. For us, it marked a new experience—same school, same uniforms albeit different years, and sometimes overlapping friendships. Trinity School went out of its way to accommodate us. My brother received assistance from two male English students to help him settle in, and I was paired with two female students: Kate, an English girl who was tall, skinny, and with over-the-shoulder blonde hair, and Rahana, a Bangladeshi British student with long black hair and a round face. Both were incredibly supportive and always willing to lend a hand whenever I needed help. Their kindness left a lasting impression on me, and I remain grateful for their guidance during my time at Trinity.

Mrs. Maureen Lovett, an older lady, was appointed to assist me with my classes and English language skills. She was exceptionally kind and spoke with a clear, beautiful English accent. Fair-skinned with short, wavy blonde hair, she may have appeared stern to others, but to me, she was a gentle soul with the patience of a saint, ensuring I adjusted well. She resembled a caring grandmother who cherished every moment spent with her grandchild. Mrs. Lovett was straightforward and occasionally joined me in class to ensure I had no language difficulties, especially since I was enrolled a year ahead of my expected level. I quickly thrived at school, receiving commendations, winning prizes, and only entering the headteacher's office to receive congratulations for my academic achievements.

The uniform was a surprise, but I enjoyed wearing it. It was black trousers, a white shirt, a green jumper with a school emblem on the left side, and a tie in all three colours. Shoes were always black, and you could not wear anything else. Even Physical Education had a uniform: a green pleated wraparound skirt, a white short-sleeve shirt, and white trainers, the only time we were allowed to wear them. Uniform was a great representation of the schooling system in the UK. The school was massive, with an even bigger field where most sports day events occurred. We also had an enormous swimming pool for Physical Education and school competitions.

Physical Education was always fun because we got to play rounders, which was new to me but was basically like baseball. We also played basketball, which my Physical Education teacher thought I'd excel at because of my height. I enjoyed it, and every sports day, I participated in the speed-walking competition since I could walk really fast. The adrenaline rush from that was incredibly exciting! It was a fun activity with the whole school present. A year above mine, Husein's friends were mainly boys, and all wanted to learn the unsavoury Bosnian words, which my brother seemed to oblige. But still there was a lot of laughter during sports days. Everyone was always in good spirits. It was a time when we forgot that we were refugees.

I also studied French, which Mary taught. She was a strict teacher but a nice person. I admit, I wish I had paid more attention in her classes, because maybe my French would be better now. Like every other teacher, she knew my brother and I were refugees. We were the only refugees in the entire school, so we had a cool kid status amongst our peers, though there was nothing cool about being a refugee. I remember once, during Parents Evening, Mary and my father spoke but not about me. She wanted her family and ours to meet for dinner at their house. She had a son and a daughter. Ben was my age, and Ruth was my brother's, two years older than me. Their father, Mary's husband, Tim, was a tall, bearded artist with shaggy golden-brown hair and glasses and equally as nice and welcoming.

It developed into a beautiful friendship. We would go to their house for dinner, and they would come to ours. Ben and Ruth loved Bosnian food, and Mama always made extra. Mary had a sister who lived in the countryside close to Southampton, and we were invited there for a long weekend. If I thought Northampton was cold, this was ten times worse, and wet. I'll never forget the photo we took that day. Everyone else looked perfectly fine, and then there's me, shivering like I'd been stranded in Antarctica with nothing but skin and bones! But it was a great change of scenery. On that trip, I shared a room with Ruth, my brother with Ben, and we all got on. And yes, we got up to mischief, but that was part of growing up. I vividly remember the day Ben decided to show off his unicycle skills and generously let us all have a go. He rode that thing like he'd been born on one wheel whereas I looked like a giraffe trying to roller skate. It was all about balance, but with just one wheel! I kept toppling over like a human Jenga tower, despite Ben's heroic attempts to keep me upright.

I remember one occasion when Tim notified my father about an English/Bosnian translator job at the British Army barracks outside Northampton. My father instantly applied, and Tim offered to drive him to the interview and back. It was two interviews in total, and Tim was happy to help. But at the job interview was also a Bosnian Serb woman who lived in Northampton with her family. Her English was nowhere near as fluent my father's because she had learned conversational English in Northampton, where she had lived less than a year, but in Bosnia, she was a teacher of the Serbo-Croat language.

The job was given to her. Tim was shocked. Mama remembers Tim's reaction: "How could they give it to her when her English isn't close to what yours is?"

Unfortunately, the politics of the British government in the 1990s was to accept everything Serbian, even if the quality was poor. My father, who was even an expert on Shakespearian language and could translate the old language and was an interpreter for UNPROFOR in Croatia, was not offered the job.

Our lives continued in Northampton. My brother and I went to school, Mama studied English and looked after our home, and my father buried himself in the events of the war.

LJILJAN

Set on white paper with purple heading, *Ljiljan* was the journalistic answer to the defence of the Bosnian people and our country. It was a weekly political newspaper founded and edited by Dr Dzemaludin Latic. The Iranian government financed the newspaper's existence. Its establishment came after a newspaper called *Muslimanski Glas* (*The Muslim Voice*), established by the SDA, was pulled out of nationwide circulation and was published only in the besieged Sarajevo. Then the two newspapers, *Muslimanski Glas* and *Ljiljan*, merged in 1993. This weekly newspaper was published in part of Bosnia that was considered free territory, and then also in the diaspora, from Türkiye to England, except in Croatia, because Tudjman banned it as soon as the HVO attacked the Army of the Republic of Bosnia and Herzegovina. *Ljiljan* exposed the goals of Milosevic and Tudzman, both of whom sought to ethnically cleanse Bosniaks and partition Bosnia amongst themselves.

My father was part of the army of *Ljiljan* correspondents who told the story of what was happening in Bosnia and how the West prevented us from defending ourselves. How he got involved with the paper, I do not know, but it started in Northampton. He wrote a review of the British press and conducted interviews with various people. He interviewed *The Guardian* newspaper's Ed Vulliamy; Dr Francis Boyle, an American professor and human rights lawyer who was also legal counsel for Bosnia during the war; Noel Malcolm, the author of *Bosnia: A Short History*, and many others. My parents regularly attended any protest held in London for Bosnia. I remember Mama telling me that when at Trafalgar Square in London during one demonstration she was handing out leaflets about the war in Bosnia. Upon witnessing this, Malcolm told her not to go alone as there were Serbian counter-protestors who might attack her. He then asked two of his colleagues to accompany Mama and help her hand out the leaflets. There were so many important figures from public life who saw the injustice of what was happening and took to the streets to call for the end of the war. If those voices could have taken the reins of British government for a day, I believe the war would never have lasted for as long as it had.

In mid-1993, after we'd been in the UK for three months, Islamic and Arab countries frustrated by the ongoing massacres in Bosnia and the lack of Western intervention ramped up sending weapons and humanitarian aid. The US played a significant role in the airlift of these weapons, using its C-130 Hercules aircraft.[11] Weapons purchased by Iran and Türkiye, with financial backing from Saudi Arabia, were first transported to Croatia by Iran's national carrier, Iran Air, and later via a fleet of black C-130 Hercules.[12] Pakistan defied the arms embargo they called illegal as their intelligence agency airlifted anti-tank guided missiles for Bosnia.[13] The United Arab Emirates, apart from taking part in peacekeeping efforts and delivering humanitarian aid both during the war and in its aftermath, was one of the earliest non-NATO countries to voice its backing for NATO's air campaign.[14] King Hussein of Jordan provided humanitarian aid and urged for international support for the Bosniaks. Meanwhile, Malaysia, led by Prime Minister Mahathir Mohamad, provided significant humanitarian assistance and accepted Bosnian refugees. He also sent a contingent of soldiers to participate in UN peacekeeping operations to help stabilise the situation in Bosnia.[15]

Around this time, I would sit in the living room, listening to my parents and various connections discuss the planes coming in to help Bosnians. I felt an overwhelming sense of pride and deep gratitude for those who selflessly came together to ease the suffering of the Bosnian people. In those moments, it felt like humanity had truly prevailed. I was especially thankful for the Arab and Islamic countries that stood up for Bosnia, even calling in their debts with the Americans to help. The war had dragged on for far too long, filled with unimaginable horrors—killing, raping, and endless suffering—and it felt like there was finally a glimmer of hope. The actions of the United States and Muslim countries, but in particular Saudi King Fahd acting as a staunch ally and lobbyist in Washington on behalf of Bosnia[16], enabled the Bosnian Army to reclaim significant territories initially occupied by Serbs at the start of the war. But it was also the strategy, courage, and determination of the Bosnian Army, combined with those weapons, that prevented many more atrocities.

In the UK, public opinion diverged sharply from their Foreign Office, known for its steadfast support of the Serbs.

Brendan Simms's book, *Unfinest Hour: Britain and the Destruction of Bosnia*, delves into this period, detailing the war's progression, unfolding events, and the contentious debates that pitted US Senators and Congressmen such as Sen. Bob Dole, Sen. John McCain, Sen. Joe Lieberman, Congressman Frank McCloskey, etc., advocating for Bosnia against the British Conservative Party, which largely opposed intervention. A notable figure within the Conservative Party who broke ranks was Lord Patrick Cormack, a former Member of Parliament. Horrified by the atrocities in Bosnia, Cormack was among the first MPs to advocate for British military involvement. He actively supported Western intervention against the Bosnian Serbs, and he chaired parliamentary groups dedicated to Bosnia's cause.

My parents met Lord Cormack in Parliament at an event he organised for Bosnia. Mama told me that my father noticed a painting and wanted to photograph it for his article. Mama reminded him that taking photos in Parliament was not allowed. Lord Cormack, overhearing their conversation, smiled and told my father, "You should listen to your wife. She is right." Later, Lord Cormack bent the rules and allowed my father to take the photo.

The other most evident support for Bosnia was when mothers with their children in prams came to Trafalgar Square to protest to end the war. British public support for arming Bosnians was strong. I would regularly see newspapers in shops filled with images of bombings and concentration camps. My father wrote about all this. Bosnians and our country's supporters, and especially foreign diplomats, regularly read his articles.

Ljiljan dominates my memories of Northampton. I'll always remember the white fax machine's receiver constantly in my father's hand. Or the thermal printing paper that would roll out of the fax machine, coming from Sarajevo, the US, the UK, or some other place. That fax machine was a constant presence. I also remember the muffled sound as my father spoke to Dr Latic, who was in Sarajevo. The phone line was sometimes bad, but they managed to communicate albeit both were shouting into the phone receiver as if trying to hear each other from across a motorway. The usual between the two was "Can you hear me?" and I would be sitting in the living room witnessing this and silently responding as if I was a soldier and its question was aimed at me: "Loud and clear, Sir."

My father's involvement with *Ljiljan* meant that he and Mama travelled to London regularly. When that proved a financial strain, they decided we should all leave Northampton at the end of the school year in 1995. I only had a year left of school, and I was not thrilled at the prospect. But it was not down to me.

My final day was sad. But in comparison to leaving Zagreb, where I was bullied and unwelcome, leaving Trinity School was much better. So many photos were taken, and so many teachers and friends to say goodbye to. Although I would miss my friends, I would also miss Mrs Lovett. She was a major part of my year nine at school. I still sometimes saw her in year ten, but not as an extra teacher, more so socially or in passing at school. I truly believe her contribution to my studies in year nine made a profound difference. She took the time to sit with me, patiently going over my homework, and when I struggled to understand something, she'd ask me to read it aloud and describe what I thought it meant. She guided me through English grammar and sentence structuring, and much of my early writing skills can be credited to her support. The way she spoke was always so eloquent, ensuring I heard every word pronounced clearly, every letter sounded out perfectly. That attention to detail was invaluable, especially since I had never studied in an English-speaking school before.

My fourth school for the final year was odd. The school was different, and the students were not as warm as those in Trinity School. I didn't enjoy this school and missed my friends from Northampton. The only thing that kept me going was the constant letters we exchanged. They would fill me in on all the latest gossip, while I shared stories about my new school, where despite my efforts, I had only made a couple of friends. I understood why we moved to London, but I wasn't thrilled about it. But I loved my humanities class because I had a good teacher who encouraged my work on the conflict in Bosnia and thought it would benefit me as I wanted to be a journalist. For one of the assignments, counted as an exam, I was asked if I would like to write an essay about the war in Bosnia and what led to that point. I did that and got an A star for that exam. The teacher thought it was the most well described and written, and I was told he enjoyed reading it, as did the entire exam board.

As I immersed myself in studying the Bosnian War for my exams, my parents continued to show their deep concern by attending events related to our homeland. But this period also marked the beginning of challenges in their relationship. My father's intense focus on Bosnia seemed to transform him, making him more controlling and quick-tempered, even over minor issues. His presence at home diminished, while Mama worked tirelessly to maintain the family's stability and harmony.

I could see how much Mama was juggling: taking care of me and my brother, keeping the household in order, and staying informed about the conflict in Bosnia. Despite everything, her resilience was striking. I felt myself drawing closer to her, finding comfort in her steady presence. Our bond deepened over long talks. She'd listen as I shared my thoughts about the war, my studies, and my growing ambition to become a war correspondent.

Although my budding interest in politics and global events could have connected me more with my father, our interactions remained distant. I'd try to engage him in conversations about Bosnia or my future goals, but his responses were often short, his mind elsewhere. His commitment to the Bosnian cause and his work consumed most of his attention, leaving only brief, sometimes half-hearted moments when we connected. It was frustrating because I wanted more from him, but those moments rarely came.

I carried a complicated mix of feelings toward him. On one hand, I felt abandoned, wishing for a closer relationship. On the other hand, I had become so used to his absence, so aligned with Mama, that I sometimes questioned whether I even needed him to be more present. My brother, on the other hand, seemed completely absorbed in his computer programming, barely aware of the emotional distance in our family.

Music became my refuge. The raw, melancholic sounds of Nirvana spoke to me in a way nothing else did. I'd retreat to my room and lose myself in their albums, letting the music fill the emotional gaps. Basketball, once a passion, slowly fell behind as my academic interests and fascination with politics took over. Still, I'd play with friends every now and then, enjoying the escape it provided from the intensity of everything going on.

A couple of friends I had didn't share my love of music. That was part of my own world while at the same time I focussed on politics and journalism. That period of my life, although difficult, was pivotal. It laid the groundwork for who I would become. The tensions at home, my parents' involvement in the Bosnian cause, and my own academic pursuits pushed me to explore the impact of media on public understanding of war. As I dove deeper into studying the Bosnian conflict for school, I saw my parents continue their activism, and though our family dynamic was far from simple, their passion and commitment inspired me to forge my own path.

THE SPOTLIGHT

As a teenager in vibrant London, while my friends were out enjoying movies and laughter, I found myself captivated by the news, my heart racing with every report. CNN's Christiane Amanpour was my guiding star, her voice echoing through our living room as I witnessed the harrowing scenes from Bosnia. I was struck with horror, watching terrified civilians run for their lives, desperately dodging the merciless fire from Serb snipers. Even then, I felt a stirring recognition that this coverage was not just news, it was a lifeline, a raw glimpse into the truth of human suffering that many others overlooked.

My admiration for American media swelled as they relentlessly highlighted the plight of the Bosnian people. Their coverage ignited a fire within the American public, compelling countless citizens to reach out to their congressmen and the White House, demanding action. It felt like a collective heartbeat, a powerful reminder that the voices of the people could indeed influence the course of history. The support from influential figures and organisations added fuel to this fire, pushing for an end to the war. I realised that without the relentless public outcry, politicians would have remained silent, their inaction allowing the war to drag on indefinitely.

In my own home, I was surrounded by a whirlwind of passionate discussions as my parents cultivated a circle of informed friends. Around our dining table, academics and diplomats shared meals and ideas, their conversations crackling with urgency and determination. My father, now conducting interviews and stirring controversy with his writing, became a beacon of urgency. It was at that time that a US diplomat told my father that the British government was bugging our home phone.

I soaked it all in, a sponge absorbing the weight of the world around me. When Mladen, a friend of my father's, called to let him know Channel 4 News was producing a youth-focused interview on Bosnia and would I be interested to take part, I felt a rush of excitement. Without hesitation, I exclaimed, "Yes!" My father's attempts to coach me were unnecessary; I had devoured every detail of the war and its complexities, far beyond what was typical for someone my age.

As I navigated the media landscape, I became acutely aware of the brutal realities unfolding in Bosnia. Each day, I flipped through news channels, my heart heavy with the images of destruction and despair. I saw towns engulfed in death, UN personnel struggling to make a difference, and Sarajevo enduring the longest siege in the history of modern warfare. The bombs lighting up the night sky were a haunting reminder of the fragility of life.

Then came the heart-wrenching tragedy of Srebrenica in July 1995, where thousands of Bosniak men and boys were mercilessly slaughtered. The Dutch battalion, overwhelmed and under-equipped, could do nothing as the Bosnian Serb forces advanced. The denial of air support by UNPROFOR felt like a betrayal, and the massacre became a symbol of the international community's failure to protect the innocent.

On a sun-drenched September day, I walked with my father toward the ITN building, my heart racing with anticipation. This was the moment I had been waiting for: a chance to share my perspective on the Dayton Accord alongside young people from all ethnic groups. As we entered the building, I could almost see my future unfolding before me. This is where I wanted to be.

In the hair and makeup room, I met a Bosnian Croat girl who would join me on the panel. The tension was palpable. The Bosnian Serb girl, I had learned, cancelled her appearance with us, a poignant reminder of the divisions that still lingered but also served as an early example of the enduring impact of the Dayton Peace Agreement. But when I took my seat around the anchor's desk, I felt a surge of hope. Badawi, warm and gracious, made me feel at ease. This was my moment. Badawi spoke with the perfect British English I heard on the news. Until the taping began, the Bosnian Croat girl remained silent, but Badawi and I chatted amiably. Badawi asked what I wanted to study next, and I told her journalism because I wanted to be a war correspondent and then an anchor.

When the cameras rolled, I spoke with clarity and conviction. I thanked Badawi afterward, unaware that the legendary

Sir Trevor McDonald had been watching from the control room. His kind words and invitation to join him in the editing suite filled me with a sense of validation and excitement. Here I was, a fifteen-year-old girl, treated with respect and kindness by the very professionals I had long admired.

The journey that led me to that moment in the ITN building was paved with pain. Each news report, each discussion around our dining table, each image of devastation in Bosnia fuelled my determination to make a difference. I remember the nights I lay awake, my thoughts racing with the stories of those caught in the crossfire of conflict. The faces of children my age, forced to grow up too quickly in the shadow of war, haunted me. Their resilience in the face of unimaginable hardship both inspired and saddened me, igniting a fierce desire to share their stories with the world.

As I stood in the ITN building, surrounded by the buzz of a working newsroom, a surge of excitement coursed through my veins. This was the world I wanted to be part of, a world where words could shine a light on injustice, where stories could move people to action. The thrill of being amid it all was intoxicating, filling me with a sense of purpose I had never experienced before.

Yet, even in that moment of triumph, a shadow of sadness lingered. I thought of the Bosnian Serb girl who had refused to join us, a stark reminder of the deep-seated divisions that the war had created. How could we hope for peace when the wounds were still so raw, when young people like us couldn't even sit in the same room together?

But with that sadness came a renewed sense of determination. If we, the youth, couldn't bridge these divides, who could? I vowed then and there to use whatever platform I might gain in the future to foster understanding, to give voice to the voiceless, and to challenge the narratives that perpetuated conflict.

As Sir Trevor shared his wisdom with me in the editing suite, I felt the weight of responsibility settling on my shoulders. This wasn't just about pursuing a career, it was about carrying forward the torch of truth and compassion that journalists such as Amanpour, Badawi, and Sir Trevor held high.

Looking back on that day, I am filled with a bittersweet nostalgia. The excitement of that first taste of the journalism world still lingers, as does the sadness for all that was lost in the war. But above all, I was overwhelmed by a passionate commitment to the ideals that were forged in those tumultuous years.

I knew that the world of journalism could be harsh and unforgiving. But the kindness shown to me by Badawi and Sir Trevor had given me hope—hope that there was still room in this industry for compassion, for integrity, for the pursuit of truth above all else.

When I left the ITN building that day, stepping back into the bustling streets of London, I carried with me a fire that would never be extinguished. The horrors of Bosnia had shaped me, the power of media had inspired me, and the kindness of those journalists had shown me the kind of professional I wanted to become.

The world was waiting, with all its complexities and conflicts, its triumphs and tragedies. And I was ready to tell its stories, armed with the passion of youth, the wisdom gained from witnessing war, and an unwavering commitment to the truth. The journey ahead would be challenging, but I was prepared to face it head-on, carrying with me the lessons learned in those formative years, years that had taught me the true power of words, the importance of bearing witness, and the profound impact that honest, compassionate journalism could have on the world.

NUMB

It had been almost a year since the signing of the Dayton Accord, which ended nearly four years of brutal war in Bosnia. The conflict claimed over 100,000 lives, including more than 8,000 during the Srebrenica Genocide. Between 20,000 and 50,000 people—girls, women, and men—were raped, including my aunt. Thousands were still missing, with mass graves still undiscovered. Over two million people, including my family, were displaced, marking the Bosnian War as the worst conflict in Europe since World War II. The devastation of the infrastructure had significantly slowed economic recovery, and Bosnia was reliant on international funding from the US, the EU, and the Middle East.

Many Bosnian refugees were staying put in the countries they fled to, but there were also those who wanted to go back as soon as possible. My father was one of them. Eager for us to return, he made the decision without consulting any of us, not even Mama. Their marriage was at breaking point, and he assumed he should make decisions on her behalf.

The warm September evening in 1996 was suffocating inside our London terraced house, thick with tension as the conversation about returning to Bosnia spiralled into a heated argument. He had made up his mind, but the three of us stood against him. I told him I wanted to stay in London, my voice steady but laced with defiance. His reaction was instant: pure fury. I watched as he angrily unbuttoned his pastel-blue shirt cuffs, rolling up his sleeves with a deliberate, sharp motion. The air between us felt electric, heavy, like the charged silence before a fight. I stared at him, heart pounding, bracing myself, trying to read his next move.

Despite my vigilance, I was unprepared for what came next. In a flash of anger, my father's dark eyes blazed and his teeth clenched. The sudden impact of his palm against my right ear left me gasping. The sharp sting radiated through my cheek, a burning sensation spreading across my face and down to the neckline of my white top.

The shock was palpable. This wasn't just a physical blow, it was a shattering of trust and safety. Our living room, once a place of family gatherings and lively discussions about world events, had suddenly become a battleground. The contrast between the warmth of the Indian summer outside and the cold reality inside our home was stark.

As I stood there, my ear throbbing and my face burning, I felt a mix of emotions wash over me. Confusion, hurt, and anger swirled together, challenging everything I thought I knew about my family and my place in it. The man who had encouraged my interest in world affairs, who had proudly walked me into the ITN building just months before, now stood before me as someone I barely recognised.

This moment marked a turning point, not just in my relationship with my father but also in my understanding of the complexities of human nature. The passion that had driven him to fight for justice in Bosnia had somehow morphed into this uncontrolled anger at home. It was a harsh lesson in the duality of human character, how someone could be both an advocate for peace and a source of conflict.

As the heat from the slap slowly subsided, I realised that the world I had been so eager to understand and report on was not just "out there" in far-off war zones, but right here in my own home. The complexities of human relationships, the impact of stress and trauma, and the fragility of peace were all playing out in miniature within our family.

When I touched the spot on my ear that throbbed with pain, droplets of blood clung to my fingertips. My earring—half of the pair I've worn since childhood—was gone, leaving behind a painful tear through my earlobe. These small gold hoops, each adorned with a tiny gold and red emerald, have been one of the few constants in my tumultuous life. I'd never once removed them. But as I shook with a mixture of indignation and resolve, I was more determined than ever.

"No!" I shouted, my voice echoing through our small London home. "I will not go to Bosnia with you." At fifteen, I had nearly reached my full height of six foot one. I didn't fear him, though this was the first time he'd struck me. It took a moment for the reality of what had happened to sink in.

My brother Husein, seventeen and solidly built at 80 kilos, sprang into action. He shoved our father to the floor, sending him sprawling between the fireplace and an armchair. My ear still buzzed from the impact, and the sound of his fall barely registered. But I saw him there, on the floor, his eyes blazing with a rage that seemed to want to consume me.

As my father rose, rebuffed by both his children, he turned his wrath toward Mama. Their confrontation, though purely verbal, was vicious and prolonged. It was fought with a ferocity reminiscent of the Serb forces against our Bosnian countrymen. In recent months, my father's anger had reached a fever pitch, with the thin walls of our attached house offering our neighbours unwanted insight into my parents' crumbling relationship. These constant disputes, coupled with my father's controlling nature, had irreparably damaged their marriage. That late evening skirmish was the worst yet.

My father was hell-bent on our family returning to Bosnia, to a country that would be unrecognisable to us now. The Dayton Accord had somewhat stemmed the bloodshed in December 1995, but it hadn't truly ended the war, merely frozen it, ready to erupt in some other form later. Although my father may have deemed it "safe" to return, Mama—ever the pragmatist—understood all too well that Bosnia's infrastructure remained as ravaged as its people.

That evening, Husein had come to my aid. He promised to stay with Mama and me in London rather than return to Sarajevo with our father. That night, at least, Husein, Mama, and I formed a united front. Our father encamped downstairs, while Mama moved into my room, and Husein retreated to his own. If Mama and I felt cramped amidst the tall shelves of world literature our family had amassed and the hulking brown desk where I did my homework, neither of us voiced a complaint.

Perhaps these early alliances already foretold the outcome of our family's private war. Even that first night, Husein chose the comfort and familiarity of his larger room, where he logged on to his computer and played games. Mama and I lay awake in my double bed, the silence between us heavy with unspoken fears and determination. Downstairs, my father stayed up through the night, chain-smoking and drinking whiskey, with only the blaring TV for company.

The following morning, a sombre haze hung in the air, equal parts stale cigarette smoke and the residue of my family's collective emotions. My father made no apologies, nor did he attempt to have a civil discussion. With battle lines drawn, we ate breakfast in shifts: first Husein and our father, then Mama and me.

Later that day, I accompanied Mama to her appointment with a divorce lawyer, whose office was about a half-hour walk from our house. The marriage had been broken for some time. Perhaps the fissures were there even before the war, before we became a family of refugees, never quite believing we were safe and certainly never feeling that we belonged, that we were home.

My father's violent outburst had not been his first. Their arguments had started long before our move to London, but the most recent ones always revolved around his demand that Mama go back to Bosnia with him, that we return there as a family. One night, Mama told him she wanted a divorce. His response was chilling. He said he would kill her if she left him.

Years later, Mama confided in me that she'd considered leaving our father when Husein and I were just toddlers. My father—like many Bosnian men—subscribed to the traditional views of our country's patriarchal society. In Brcko,

Mama worked full-time as a bookkeeper, made all our meals, looked after our home and our family. All of this, while my father hosted boisterous drinking parties for his university colleagues and old classmates late into the night. Mama's fear that my father would deploy his vast network of contacts should she file for divorce, potentially cutting off her access to me and Husein, had kept her trapped for years.

But after my father's latest outburst, Mama was finally determined to go through with the divorce. We walked to the lawyer's office together, Mama as elegant as ever with her light brown hair cut in a sleek French bob. She looked as though she should be strolling along a tree-lined Paris avenue rather than a London street. Not knowing what would happen next, she held her head high, walking with purpose.

In the lawyer's office, I recounted my father's threat. The lawyer advised Mama that she needed a restraining order, which would be issued shortly.

While Mama and I were at her lawyer's, my father managed to manipulate my brother, promising him castles in the sky if he returned to Bosnia. The reality was the complete opposite, but my father wanted two things: to hurt Mama and to force her to return to Bosnia. Mama begged Husein to stay and finish his education in England and get a British passport, and then he could go wherever he wanted. But his mind was made up. The week before their departure, my father had gifted me £100. The day before he left, he demanded I return it. I did.

I can still picture the multi-coloured September leaves lying in piles beside our neighbours' gardens. Inside, I see my father collecting a few small pieces of furniture from our rented London house. I lean against the doorframe of the kitchen, and from here, I can see into the living room—the brown sofa and armchairs, the wooden coffee table with its smooth surface, my father's ashtray now empty. I watch my father pacing, a cigarette in his right hand, while Husein gathers his things. My father wears a black windbreaker, jeans, and casual shoes. He looks as though he might be going out for one of his habitual walks.

I waited for my father to say goodbye to me, to perhaps whisper an apology or, at the very least, to acknowledge my presence. He did not do any of this.

And then, just like the night my father struck me, Husein came on stage to play his role. He hugged Mama and then me before walking out the door behind our father. Outside, my father and brother got into the van—part of a humanitarian convoy our father had summoned—and they drove away.

For Mama and me, life changed overnight. In the wake of my father's and brother's departure, everything became very difficult. But in the weeks and months that followed, Mama proved herself the warrior she had always been. During the heady days of my father's war efforts, when he mingled with intellectuals, diplomats, journalists, and activists, Mama had not only stood by her husband but had added her own insights and opinions. Now, her final decision to divorce our father was one of survival.

In the lead-up to the divorce, my father made his own decisions, choices surely based on his survival but also designed to punish both Mama and me. He left us with no means of financial support, refusing to transfer crucial documents from his name to Mama's. These papers were essential for her to register for a National Insurance (NI) number so that she could look for work. It would take Mama's herculean effort to navigate the seemingly endless bureaucratic maze to make these changes.

The very day my father and brother left London, Mama marched us into the Job Centre. There, we were informed that her application for an NI number was being processed. Without this, Mama would be unable to work. Day after day, we returned to that lifeless government building, its interior and façade matching the dull expressions of most who worked there.

But there was one exception. One day, after waiting in the usual queue, Mama explained our situation to a middle-aged British Indian clerk. He rifled through the paperwork and immediately declared ours an "emergency case." Within thirty-six hours, Mama was issued an NI number and was actively job hunting.

Mama's efforts and this important victory brought with it an unexpected consequence. Soon after, she received a letter informing her of her responsibility to repay a loan my father had taken out just after we'd moved to our last family home in London. He had never told us about this debt. The information came like a gut-punch. Why would he do such a thing?

In the days just before he and Husein left, Mama had transferred her share of ownership in our Brcko apartment to Husein so that he could use these funds for a place to live in Sarajevo. Yes, our father would live there too. Her intent was to provide for her son.

In one sense, my father treated Mama and me as casualties of war, left behind and discarded. He managed to sell the Brcko apartment and buy a new one in Sarajevo, ironically, the same apartment he had lived in as a student, some twenty minutes walking distance from Bascarsija, Sarajevo's historic marketplace. My father gifted his share of the apartment to Husein as well.

But nothing justified what he did to Mama and me by having us pay his debt. What sort of man does that to his family, to his child? Or in his spitefulness, did he no longer consider us his family? I often wondered.

He had one face amongst his friends who idolised him. His other face, his true face, was that of a bully, egomaniac, and a liar. He had hoped that we wouldn't succeed and would come running after him. How little he thought of us.

To make matters worse, he started telling everyone who would listen anything he could fabricate against Mama and me. He lied to gain sympathy and paint himself as the victim. A victim he was not.

The battle lines were very clear: Mama and me on one side, my father and my brother on the other. In this war of attrition, we were determined to not just survive but to thrive, despite the obstacles my father had so callously placed in our path.

THE NIGHTMARE

The nightmares began just before my brother and father left, a sinister prelude to the fracturing of our family. At first, I couldn't comprehend their meaning, despite their vivid clarity. The repetition haunted me, night after night, for almost a year.

It was a toxic brew of war images from Bosnia splashed across newspapers, the endless paperwork my father left strewn about, and my own insatiable curiosity that fed this nightly horror. My eagerness to understand the adult world around me had betrayed me, plunging me into a realm of fear I was ill equipped to navigate.

As I closed my eyes, I could see it all unfold with terrifying clarity. The dream always began the same way: I stood in a sea of golden wheat, its beauty made almost painful by the intensity of the sunlight. A slow wind caressed the stalks, creating a gentle rustling that should have been soothing. Instead, it filled me with an inexplicable dread.

I moved through the field, trying to play the part of an intrepid explorer, a female Indiana Jones, I told myself. But the façade of bravery crumbled quickly. The spaces between the wheat rows began to narrow, closing in on me like the walls of a shrinking room. The slants of sunlight bent swiftly, casting long shadows that seemed to reach for me with grasping fingers.

My skin prickled with goosebumps despite the warmth, and I shivered uncontrollably. Suddenly, shouting erupted behind me, guttural and filled with menace. Panic seized me, and I ran, my feet clumsy and uncooperative. I tripped, my hands grasping foolishly at the swaying wheat for support. As I hit the ground, an invisible weight crushed down on my chest, leaving me paralysed and gasping for air. I tried to scream, but no sound escaped my lips. I was mute, helpless, trapped in my own body.

Two beams of light cut through the wheat, heralding the approach of a vehicle. It barrelled toward me, and my heart pounded so violently I feared it might burst from my chest. The black Jeep emerged from the parting wheat, and I could see the men inside, their faces twisted with cruel intent. The air filled with acrid petrol fumes, so intense it made my stomach churn.

In a disorienting shift, bright lights surrounded me, reminiscent of harsh stage lighting. A skyscraper materialised. I recognised it as the building where we lived in our first apartment in Brcko. Peering out the window, I saw another building where one of my paternal aunts lived. It loomed impossibly close, swaying like the wheat in an unnatural wind. The structure leaned closer still, so near that I could have reached out and touched it if I dared.

Desperate for escape, I raced to another window. Below, I saw the square where I played as a child. But it was wrong somehow, distorted, threatening. The familiar had become alien and dangerous.

In another jarring transition, I found myself on the ground again. The surface beneath me was hard and cold, a stark contrast to the earlier wheat field. The black Jeep skidded to a stop before me, its headlights blinding me with their glare. For a moment, I was lost in a world of searing white light and paralysing fear.

Then I was running again, my legs pumping furiously but making no progress. It's as if I was on a nightmarish treadmill, the darkness around me absolute and oppressive. The Jeep's engine roared, growing louder as it gained on me. It skidded to a stop once more, and four men leaped from the vehicle. Their hands reached for me, fingers like claws, and just as they were about to seize me—

I would wake up, drenched in sweat, my hair plastered to my face. My heart thundered in my chest, and it took what felt like hours for the adrenaline to subside. Each night, as I lay in bed, I wondered with growing dread if the nightmare would return. The fear of sleep becomes almost as terrifying as the dream itself.

This nightly torment persisted, an unwelcome bedfellow, until one day it simply…stopped. Not because the fear had subsided or because I had conquered some inner demon. No, it stopped because I made a conscious choice to leave the war behind, to turn away from the horrors that had become so familiar, and because Mama had spent her free time with me taking me to museums where my mind turned toward the beauty of historic paintings and literature.

In the light of day, I could rationalise the nightmare's elements: the wheat fields of my homeland, now tainted by conflict; the Jeep, a symbol of the militarisation that had torn my country apart; the familiar buildings of my childhood, made strange and threatening by the ravages of war. But in the dark of night, logic held no sway over the primal fear that gripped me.

The nightmare was a manifestation of all I had seen and heard, all that I feared might come to pass. It was my young mind's attempt to process the destruction of my home, the fracturing of my family, the loss of innocence that comes with witnessing the cruelties of war, even from afar.

As I grew older, I came to understand that the nightmare was also a reflection of my own internal conflict. The wheat field represented the beauty and peace of my past, while the menacing Jeep and its occupants symbolised the violent intrusion of war into that idyllic scene. The familiar buildings, made strange and threatening, mirrored my sense of displacement and the loss of the secure world I had once known.

The paralysis I experienced in the dream—the inability to scream, to run effectively—was perhaps the most telling aspect. It represented my feelings of helplessness in the face of forces far beyond my control or understanding. As a child caught in the crossfire of adult conflicts and global politics, what power did I have to change my circumstances?

Yet, in choosing to leave the war behind, in refusing to let the nightmare continue its reign over my subconscious, I took my first step toward reclaiming that power. It was a small act of defiance against the fear and uncertainty that had dominated my young life.

The nightmares may have faded, but their impact lingered. They served as a reminder of the resilience of the human spirit, of our capacity to endure and overcome even the most terrifying of circumstances.

In the end, the choice to leave the war behind was not just about escaping nightmares. It was about embracing hope, about believing in the possibility of a future unmarred by the shadows of the past. It was the first step on a long journey of healing and self-discovery.

PART III (1998–2005)

OVERCOMING

Mama and I moved into a Victorian house split into maisonettes, which was a delightful blend of modern comfort and classic charm with large rooms. We were upstairs, and our neighbour George, a World War II veteran, was downstairs. Although we each had our own entrance, we shared a garden. Shortly after we settled in, we knocked on his door to introduce ourselves. George was an older, frail gentleman who relied on a Zimmer frame for mobility. He was kind and well-spoken, and often very chatty, but one had to speak loudly for him to hear. He warmly welcomed us, saying, "Whatever you need, knock on my door, and I will help in any way I can." He also said that he never used the garden, so we were welcome to the whole thing. George exemplified selflessness in every interaction. His ever-present smile and kindness shone through, even as he faced challenges with mobility and hearing.

Mama often cooked extra food for George, knowing that he depended on meals-on-wheels, which were provided for those who lived independently but couldn't shop for and prepare meals themselves. She would say, "He should have some well-cooked comfort food." She prepared Bosnian dishes like stuffed peppers, sarma, roast chicken, and other dishes. Either I would deliver the meals, or Mama would take them herself. George was always deeply grateful. Occasionally, he would ask me or Mama to buy him newspapers, and we would happily oblige.

I cherished our conversations. George shared captivating stories from his time in the army, offering a rare glimpse into the past through the eyes of a World War II veteran. Listening to him recount those experiences felt like an honour, especially since my own life was intertwined with the echoes of war. His perspective provided a refreshing break from my own memories.

Engaging with George was not just about sharing stories; it was about connecting with history and humanity. His selflessness and ability to find joy in small moments left a lasting impression on me.

Living on that street with neighbours like George brought a sense of calm and happiness that truly made a difference and fostered a sense of community that made our street feel like home. We attended barbecue parties that felt reminiscent of life in Bosnia. The atmosphere was vibrant, filled with laughter and warmth, much like the gatherings I had experienced there. Each barbecue brought back memories of the rich culinary traditions and the communal spirit that defined those moments. The sizzling meat on the grill and the shared stories around the table created a sense of connection that transcended distance and time.

During this time, Mama was working as an optician. Her Yugoslav education wasn't recognised, so she had to requalify. She chose the optical industry because she had developed an interest in it. Meanwhile, I was studying for a BTEC Diploma in Art & Design (Media) at the University of the Arts London (UAL) and working Sundays in a department store. This gig gave me some pocket money and a delightful sense of independence.

At UAL, I had two lecturers: Paul, an Englishman, and Jim, a Scot. These two were like the Batman and Robin of the academic world. Inseparable! And if they weren't together, they always knew where the other was. Paul was the first person I met when I went for an interview in the UAL basement. Then I met Jim too. Whereas Paul spoke with a clear English accent, Jim had a heavy Scottish brogue. Having lived in the UK for five years by that point, various British accents were like music to my ears, so I had no trouble understanding Jim, but some international students suffered in understanding him, so they would often sit around me and copy my notes.

I had an amazing group of friends, each bringing a unique flavour to our adventures. My circle included British Jamaican S.W., and Japanese Tomoko and Yuki. Among them, I spent a lot of time with S.W. She was always so cheerful. Like me, she was thin, with shoulder-length hair. Hers was in braids, mine always down on my shoulders. She had a serious love for trainers, which sometimes bordered on obsessive. I remember how, despite my love for politics and music, I was utterly captivated by French fashion. I lived by Coco Chanel's mantra: "A girl should be two things: classy and fabulous." My wardrobe was always stylish, and I made it a point to keep my nails perfectly manicured, which I did myself. Shoes were my go-to. The thought of wearing trainers just didn't fit into my vision of myself at that time.

Even in winter, I opted for skirts, dresses, and jeans, embracing the chicness of it all. Although S.W. and I may not have matched in fashion sense, our friendship was perfectly in sync, and that connection brought me joy. Each gathering felt like a celebration of style and camaraderie, making those moments truly memorable.

Even more time was spent with my Japanese friends, Tomoko and Yuki. From the start, Yuki and I bonded over our shared love for the band Aerosmith, which drew us closer, with Tomoko soon joining in. Yuki was always the sensible one. She cooked only Japanese food and answered the phone with a cheerful "moshi moshi," no matter who was on the other end. Her strong accent and infectious smile made her wonderfully unique. Tomoko, on the other hand, had long black hair and a bit of a tomboy streak. She introduced me to dim sum, a delicious Chinese brunch dish that I love to this day.

I discovered Aerosmith through their song "I Don't Want to Miss a Thing" from the *Armageddon* movie soundtrack. Mama bought me my first CD single as she obviously understood my newfound love of the band, and I quickly became a devoted fan, listening to their music religiously. The song struck a chord with me, making me want to fully embrace life and not miss a thing. So, when Aerosmith announced a Toxic Twin Towers Ball concert at Wembley Stadium London toward the end of the year at UAL, my Japanese contingent and I eagerly bought tickets and were joined by other Japanese friends Tomoko and Yuki knew and with whom I quickly became friends too.

By this time, the weight of Bosnia's war-torn past hung heavy on my soul, a burden I longed to shed. As the conflict faded into history, my interest in the region's tumultuous politics began to wane, like autumn leaves drifting from once-vibrant trees. The echoes of gunfire and screams had quieted, replaced by an uneasy peace that settled over the scarred landscape.

Yet, even as I yearned for freedom from the constant reminders of that brutal war, a part of me remained tethered to the land of my ancestors. The ongoing strife in Kosovo, and Milosevic's indictment by the International Criminal Tribunal for the former Yugoslavia (ICTY), served as painful reminders of the region's unhealed wounds. I desperately sought to escape the label of being a refugee that had defined me for so long, to breathe without the suffocating memories of conflict.

In the depths of my heart, a flame of curiosity still burned, longing to know what was happening in my homeland. But it was no longer the all-consuming fire that had driven me during my school days. The passion had dimmed, replaced by a weary resignation.

It was during this time of inner turmoil that news reached Mama and me of my Uncle Huso's passing. My father's brother, a man who had once embodied the warmth and vitality of our family gatherings, had succumbed to the lingering effects of his torture in the Luka concentration camp. The vibrant soul who had weathered the storm of 1992 had finally been silenced, his spirit broken by the cruelty he had endured.

The circumstances of his death pierced my heart like a cold blade. I imagined him in his final moments, alone on a bench in Brcko, a solitary figure in a town that had once bustled with the laughter and love of our extended family.

The contrast between the lively gatherings of our past and the stark loneliness of his end was a cruel reminder of all that had been lost.

As they laid him to rest in Brcko, I found myself drowning in a sea of sorrow. Uncle Huso's fate seemed to embody the tragedy of our nation: a once-vibrant people reduced to silence, their stories ending in isolation and pain. His burial in the very soil that had witnessed both joy and unspeakable horror felt like a final, bittersweet chapter in our family's saga. Mama and I remembered him as he was before the war.

In that time of grief, I realised that no matter how far I tried to run from my past, the shadows of war would always find a way to touch my life. The story of Bosnia, of Uncle Huso, of countless others who had suffered, was etched into my very being, a sorrowful tale that would forever be a part of who I am.

And so, I was immersed in the world of rock music, which was a refuge from the shadows of the war. On the day of the Aerosmith concert, we arrived early to secure a front-row standing position. We ended up just three rows from the stage, close enough to see the band's singer Steven Tyler sweat and to recognise every facial expression Joe Perry made while playing his electric guitar.

One of the supporting acts was Lenny Kravitz, who was particularly memorable, and who I was a fan of. He exuded energy, giving us all a powerful performance, and a blend of rock, funk, soul, and R&B. His was a vibrant performance.

Despite the scorching heat, which prompted security and Wembley staff to hand out cold water in plastic cups, we had an amazing time enjoying the music and the electrifying atmosphere.

As the lights dimmed and the evening set in, Aerosmith took the stage, and Steven Tyler's iconic voice echoed through the packed Wembley Arena. We sang along to every song. By then, I could recite them all backward. I owned all their albums and had watched practically every music video they ever made. I knew Tyler's mannerisms and hand gestures for every song, and seeing his scarves adorning the microphone stand as he carried it around the stage was the ultimate moment for a music fan. There I was, singing and dancing to Aerosmith, feeling truly alive and free.

My Japanese friends later told me, "You were so full of life. You seemed like the only person there singing with Tyler." Maybe I was, because that was exactly what I needed. I needed to live, to shed the weight of the Bosnian War and everything that came with it. I wanted to be a teenager, not a daily political analyst. I didn't want to be constantly associated with everything related to that war. I wanted to enjoy my life with my friends.

I was full of life and eager to go out. When I stayed out late, I would crash at my friends' places, sparing Mama the worry of me coming home alone in the middle of the night.

She was relieved that I was finally embracing my youth and freedom—something I couldn't have done with my father around. He was far too strict. Even if Husein and I wanted to take a silly photo, he would give us a dressing down. We always had to look dead serious. When I wore a slightly cropped top, my father would tell me, "You will be cold, go change" even in the middle of summer. Now, I had the freedom to act my age and enjoy myself.

For our final university project, my friends and I decided to create a short documentary about the unsung heroes of sports—coaches, managers, and other non-celebrity figures. S.W. was a young mother, and her son's grandmother worked as an assistant to the owner of a basketball team. She helped us secure an interview with the team's coach and even chauffeured us in her boss's Bentley to Sheffield and back.

We took turns handling the camera, watched the match, and had a fantastic time. This documentary, along with my other work, led to an offer to study for a degree in journalism at the same university. I vividly recall being in a lecture theatre at UAL in the last days of my BTEC Diploma when Jim walked in, headed straight for me, and with a massive smile on his face, told me he had seen the offer in the media office. He congratulated me warmly, genuinely happy for my success. He and Paul both knew I had come to the UK as a refugee. Whenever I needed help, they provided support, references, and recommendations for my bachelor's degree. And even when I was studying for my degree, they were always happy to help.

Years later, Paul notified me that Jim had passed away too soon. I felt a sense of sadness. Jim was not only an amazing lecturer but an even better person. If there was a Scottish heaven, he'd be in it with kilted Scotsmen playing the bagpipes.

SIMPLY THE BEST

I was now studying for a bachelor's degree in journalism. Immersed so deeply in my studies, it often felt as though I was already working as a journalist. I eagerly anticipated every class, whether we were debating how different newspapers covered the same story or delving into the books assigned for our History, Politics, and Ideas class. I cherished every moment. I think I may have driven my professor a bit crazy when, halfway through the first year, I announced that I already knew my dissertation topic, which wasn't due to start until the third year. His expression was unforgettable as he said, "You have three years still, Nadina," to which I replied, "But it's best I start my research early. You know, the early bird catches the worm and all that." He rolled his eyes and responded, "OK, but please don't ask me any questions before we start the preparations." My dissertation focused on the failure to implement the Dayton Peace Agreement, which was signed almost four years prior to end the brutal war in Bosnia, and I had amassed enough research to write a book.

The idea came to me after speaking with my father. I had tried to maintain contact with him, at Mama's insistence, because she wanted me to have a relationship with him.

I kept in touch with Husein, of course, and Mama stayed connected with him as well, but not with my father. My father and I did not have the best way of communicating. He couldn't separate himself for blaming me for everything, including not joining him in Bosnia. So, our relationship wasn't a loving father-daughter relationship. It was disastrous, argumentative, to the point of him calling me names. I couldn't believe he stooped that low. That is why I wasn't always thrilled to speak with him. After any conversation we had, I felt stressed and my contempt for him grew.

Both my brother and father worked for international organisations in Sarajevo, Husein in computing and my father translating documents, a beloved hobby that had turned into his profession after returning to Bosnia. He had left *Ljiljan* back in 1997 but remained friends with the editors. My father's constant interest in the happenings in Bosnia meant he always had good information, which he frequently passed on to me while trying to get me to return to Bosnia. The information was invaluable for my dissertation, but even though my interest in Bosnia had begun to wane, I couldn't shake my curiosity, especially when it came to current and future American politics or the stories of Britain's role in the Bosnian War. But trying to get me to move to Bosnia was a losing battle. I wasn't budging.

By this point at university, I had made new friends from most corners of the world. Tomoko had temporarily gone back to Japan, whereas Yuki remained in London for another couple of years and our friendship continued with concerts, movies, and dinners.

In early 2000, Tina Turner announced her Twenty Four

Seven Millennium Tour, with a concert scheduled for July 15 at Wembley Stadium. Mama, a lifelong fan of Tina's, had always filled our home with her music. Just as with Aerosmith, I could recite Tina's lyrics backward. With Mama's birthday in August, I thought the concert tickets would make the perfect gift. I got us two tickets and eagerly awaited the gig while university life continued. During my student years, Mama was fiercely devoted to her career as an optician, a profession she grew to love. She poured her energy into caring for her patients, often coming home with the most amusing stories they shared. Mama worked tirelessly, yet she always found time to be there for me. Her job was more than just a career; it was a lifeline for the two of us. My father's battles with glaucoma meant I had to be vigilant about my own eye health, as the illness is hereditary. Mama made sure I was always in good hands, booking my appointments with doctors she worked alongside—doctors I grew to like, turning what could have been a daunting task into something I almost looked forward to. Visiting her workplace became less of a chore and more of a comforting routine, filled with familiar faces.

So, it was natural that I would make sure the day of the concert was etched in her memory too. The summer sunshine was a captivating blend of warmth and tranquillity. As the lights dimmed, anticipation electrified the air. Fans cheered and clapped, creating a buzz that rippled through the venue. As the sun descended toward the horizon, Tina stepped onto the stage. The concert kicked off with a high-energy number, Tina dancing and singing with a radiant smile. She commanded the stage with a presence like no other artist. Dressed in her signature dazzling outfits adorned with sequins and fringe, she embodied both elegance and raw power. Her voice, strong and unmistakable, soared through the venue, hitting every note with precision and passion. We sang along to every lyric like a supportive choir of voices.

Her songs told a story, and between them, she would stop to address the crowd. Her charisma was palpable, and her joy in performing was contagious. The concert was a celebration of life, love, and resilience, a testament to the power of music and the extraordinary talent of a true icon. Tina was simply the best, and there will never be another artist who could surpass her.

Music held countless meanings for me. It was the bridge that connected me to new people, breaking through cultural barriers and transporting me to a world where each note and lyric unlocked memories and emotions, much like poetry. Music was my sanctuary, a healing force that helped me escape the relentless echoes of war. It nurtured my personal growth and, most importantly, reignited a joy that had been lost since the last time I laced up my roller skates as a child in Brcko. Through music, I found the freedom to truly have fun again.

By this time, the first year of university had drawn to a close. Our Leave to Remain visas, mine and Mama's, were nearing their expiration date. The moment was approaching when we would apply for British citizenship, a milestone that loomed on the horizon like a dawn promising a new chapter.

THE INJURY

The summer of concerts had ended, and now I was embarking on the second year of university with its heavier responsibilities. I had breezed through the first year, enjoying every minute, only to return for the second with an injured knee—my sixth injury, to be precise. Basketball had been the culprit, causing a dislocation that ensured I never played again.

The winter had been cold and often slippery, forcing me to navigate the hill to the university entrance on crutches. I had never walked that slowly before, so I left my house thirty minutes earlier than usual. Reaching the entrance meant someone had to open the door for me, and inside, I would wait in the grey-walled reception area for a classmate to help me up the stairs. The building, an old newspaper publishing house, only had a goods lift requiring special signoff to use, which I couldn't be bothered to chase. So, I opted for the stairs, waiting for a friend to carry one of my crutches while I gripped the railing with my free hand.

I stopped at the desk to chat with the security guard, an Englishman in his late fifties who was always dressed in a crisp white shirt and black trousers. He reminded me of

Hector Elizondo's benevolent hotel clerk character in *Pretty Woman*. In my real-life movie, I was the injured woman on crutches, leaning against his desk while waiting for my friends to arrive. We exchanged pleasantries, grumbled about the nasty weather, and wished each other a good day.

This day was different though. The guard initiated a conversation about his work in Africa when he was younger. He told me about his time in Kenya, Zambia, and Uganda.

"Really? My father was there too. He worked in those exact same countries, as well as in the Democratic Republic of Congo and Tanzania," I said.

My response seemed to fall on deaf ears. It felt like he had a purpose in telling me this, as if there was a hidden agenda behind his words. He didn't seem interested in hearing anything from my side, almost as if he already knew. The guard didn't ask about my father's work or elaborate on his own. The brief exchange stuck in my mind though. What connected my father's career and this man's time in Africa?

After graduating from the Faculty of Philosophy at the University of Sarajevo with a degree in English Literature, my father had embarked on an international career. His friend Rizo Selmanagic, managing director of the Bosnian publishing house Svijetlost, introduced him to Emerik Blum, a Bosnian Jewish businessman, philanthropist, and founder of one of southeast Europe's largest conglomerates, Energoinvest. This multidisciplinary engineering and energy company still exists and is headquartered in Sarajevo.

Blum employed my father as a finance director and translator, shipping him to Africa in 1970. My father lived and worked there for several years, helping build transmission towers throughout Zambia, Uganda, Congo, Kenya, and Tanzania. Energoinvest provided a bodyguard for him, Steven, who would often accompany my father to bars where my father liked to buy rounds of drinks for the other patrons. Mama told me how fondly my father spoke of Steven and their long chats, and how heartbroken Steven was when my father finally left Africa and returned to Bosnia.

There were countless stories and pictures of my father with tribespeople and Bedouins from his time in places I longed to visit. As a child, my favourite tale was of him asking for directions in the vast desert. The tribesmen and Bedouins would say, "Go straight," for so and so kilometres, "then take a right." This always made me laugh, imagining an endless expanse with no buildings or markings. Bedouins, of course, rely on stars and the moon to guide them through the desert, just as the sun rises in the east and sets in the west. In my eyes, the Bedouins have the finest astronomical knowledge.

In another story, Emerik Blum arrived with his delegation from Sarajevo, and my father acted as his interpreter in Zambia. On that trip, they met with Zambia's president, Kenneth Kaunda. My father later told Mama how President Kaunda's infectious laugh rang out as he and Blum spent time with him.

In Africa, my father did meaningful work that truly made a difference in the communities. So, I couldn't help but wonder why the university's security guard felt the need to tell me about his supposed time on a continent of such extraordinary beauty and diversity.

Around the same time as my injury, Mama received a letter written in a child's handwriting in Cyrillic, the alphabet used by Serbs and a slightly different version by Russians.

The letter started, "Hi Mama..." Its contents were striking! Targeting Mama because of her adoption? What on earth was this about? I can still see the look of utter disbelief on Mama's face as she studied that letter, her expression a mix of shock and curiosity. She questioned it immediately, insisting that this letter was no coincidence. Out of all the letterboxes, it ended up in ours, and we were the only ones from the Western Balkans on the entire street. The idea that someone would dig into our past like that, going to such lengths, was downright sinister. It made us question our own safety. I must have looked at that letter countless times, unable to shake the question: Why would anyone do this? But no answer came. We didn't tell my father about it. After all, Mama didn't have that type of relationship with him to share that.

But if the letter wasn't enough, another significant memory from my university years stands out, now another crucial piece of the puzzle. I was standing in line outside the administration office to register for my second year. I opened the file given to me by one office to hand to the administrator, and a line of text jumped out: "Lives with mother on income support." That information was completely incorrect. Mama had been working since 1998 as an optical adviser. She was not on income support of any kind. As a university student, I wasn't entitled to income support either. So why would the university have such lies printed in my student files?

I was finally free. The crutches were no longer needed. Slash, the famous Guns N' Roses guitarist, had since embarked on a new venture with his band, Slash's Snakepit, aptly named given his love for snakes. Slash is an iconic figure in the world of rock music, known for his distinctive look and unparalleled talent. With his trademark top hat, dark sunglasses, and wild mane of curly hair, he cut an unforgettable silhouette on stage. His attire, typically a leather jacket and ripped jeans, embodied the quintessential rock star image. Signature songs like "Sweet Child O' Mine" and "November Rain" showcased his ability to blend technical precision with raw emotion, creating timeless rock anthems. He and his new band were scheduled to play a club gig in London.

Having been a fan of Guns N' Roses for what seemed liked forever, I was determined to interview Slash. Thus began my journey to contact his press team. I called the venue, who directed me to his recording company. They, in turn, provided the number for his press people, who wanted to know who it was for. I told them it was for a newspaper in Bosnia. These phone calls took time; none of it was a 24-hour experience. Eventually, they called back to say the interview was on. Oh wow! I thought. This was my biggest interview ever. Not even being interviewed by others had excited me as much as interviewing this living legend, Slash.

When the day finally arrived, I was as giddy as a teenager who just got their first concert tickets! Slash's laid-back and approachable demeanour contrasted sharply with the intense energy he brought to his music. We chatted casually, and he answered each question as if having a conversation with an old friend. As we wrapped up, I asked if he would ever perform in Bosnia. He said I was the first person he'd spoken to from that part of the world and that the places they hadn't been "are always the best to play in." I savoured every moment of that interview. Slash transformed from a guitarist known for classic Guns N' Roses songs into a voice that embodied graciousness and kindness. Long after our conversation, I felt that even if I never pursued a career in music journalism, at least I had the incredible experience of speaking with this legend.

The interview was published in February 2001 in Bosnia. It took me a while to come back down to earth, and my excitement was evident to my university friends. It was during this time that I struck up a new friendship with Leni, a German student who had also interviewed bands while living in France. We quickly bonded over our shared interests in music and fashion. Living near each other, we often found ourselves on the same bus to university, making us practically inseparable.

When it came to internships, I cannot recall what Leni did, but I used my Slash interview to secure an internship at TotalRock radio station in London midway through my second year. Based in West London, the station broadcasted rock and heavy metal music internationally over the internet; it continues today. The RRN Rock Radio Network preceded TotalRock, founded by a group of five. Though it was a small setup at the time, it was filled with larger-than-life personalities and had walls covered in CDs and vinyl.

Tony, one of the founders who gave me the internship, was an Englishman in his mid-fifties with white shoulder-length hair. He was often at his desk, listening to music sent to the station, as he was the one to approve the albums that came through, I believe for the content or Parental Advisory

Language labels. I spent most of my time inside the broadcast booth with the same host. One day, after assisting for a while, Tony told me I would be presenting for the afternoon. Wow, I thought, this is what you call an internship! So, that day, I took the reins. I told my brother to listen in and watch via live stream; he was at work and made everyone else follow too. We played different rock and metal bands and then received a phone call. The singer of an English heavy metal band, whose name I can't recall, liked the sound of my voice and wanted to come in and meet me.

The next day, he arrived with the entire band. He was tall with long, dark hair, dressed all in black. Not my type. Lifting his shirt, he revealed two pierced nipples. God, I thought, that must hurt. I didn't exactly look like a metalhead. No one could ever tell. It's not like I was hiding it, I just wasn't emotionally prepared to commit to a closet that looked like a goth vampire convention. I still had a deep, spiritual connection with my blue jeans and colourful tops. The band joined me and the host in the booth, turning the visit into an interview.

Shortly after this, I started dating A.L., an American guitarist my own age. He was in a California-based heavy metal band. He was almost as tall as me, and I never saw his hair because he always kept his head shaved. Our shared love for rock music brought us together after we were introduced through a friend.

We spent a lot of time in Camden Town, a vibrant and eclectic place, deeply rooted in the area's rich cultural history. As one of the world's most iconic music scenes, it offered a dynamic mix of live performances, legendary venues, and a distinctive atmosphere that attracted music lovers like us. The area had everything, from punk and goth fashion to market stalls and shops selling vintage band t-shirts, leather jackets, and other rock-inspired attire. This unique blend of music and fashion created an environment where creativity and self-expression flourished, making it particularly appealing to A.L. and me.

Camden Town held so many memories and being there with A.L. and my friends made it more special. I couldn't even count how many times I dragged Yuki to Camden, and when Tomoko was in London, she voluntarily joined the madness, S.W. and Leni too. Camden Town was the ultimate playground for trying on a new persona. They had everything, even baby bibs! So, naturally, I bought one that said, "If you think I'm cute, wait till you see my aunt," even though Husein was nowhere near getting married and having kids. I figured, someday he'll have kids, and I'll be ready to flaunt my cool aunt status.

Mama started dating Frank, a colleague from work. The first time we met, he was so nervous you'd think I was some ex-military parent minus the uniform and the arsenal of guns. I half-expected him to salute me! But he quickly recognised my down-to-earth nature and my sense of humour, which helped him relax. I felt completely at ease with him; there was never any reason not to be. He seemed genuinely nice, so who was I to judge? But the real comedy gold came when I introduced A.L. to Mama. Poor guy—A.L., the big, bad rock guitarist—was sweating buckets. He knew Mama was the main parent, so he was on his absolute best behaviour. What cracked me up the most was how he clung to my hand like it was a lifeline, even while we were sitting down. It was like he thought letting go might unleash some kind of parental wrath.

There was really no need for all those nerves, but I understood. The sight of this tough rocker, who probably spent his nights smashing guitars, getting all jittery over meeting his girlfriend's mom? Priceless. Just goes to show, even rock stars have their soft spots! And Frank, a grown man, was just as nervous to meet me. I was genuinely happy for Mama and Frank. I never imagined seeing it in a negative light. She deserved her happiness after years spent with my self-absorbed father. I kept the details of Mama's life from him because I felt it was none of his business, and I didn't share anything about my own dating life either, since we didn't have that kind of relationship.

I stayed on at TotalRock until the beginning of my third year at university, when I had to leave to focus on my dissertation. But I missed being part of the daily craziness of a live radio station and the fantastic music they played.

9/11

Now in my third and final year at university, I was finally writing my thesis after spending three years gathering a vast amount of information. On one distinctly sunny September day, I was home alone, basking in the warmth of the sun filtering through the windows. I was nestled comfortably in an armchair, positioned perfectly toward the TV so I could keep up with the latest on CNN while delving deeper into the Dayton Peace Agreement. Silence never suited me while working; I needed the hum of the news to concentrate.

But then, out of nowhere, the serene rhythm of my day was shattered. CNN broke the calm with a jarring report: A plane had crashed into the North Tower of the World Trade Centre. I gasped, feeling a chill run down my spine as disbelief gripped me. My eyes, which had been flitting between my laptop and the TV, were now locked on the screen, unable to tear away from the unfolding chaos. The volume on the TV went up, my dissertation momentarily forgotten, my laptop abandoned on the coffee table. Then, the unthinkable happened: The South Tower was hit. Within an hour, the South Tower collapsed, followed by the North Tower less than thirty minutes later.

I stayed rooted in that armchair, barely moving. For three days straight, I was transfixed by the unfolding disaster. Every detail, every update, I had to know it all. The days and months that followed became a blur of university lectures and relentless news watching. For me, the desire to be a journalist was not just about a career, it was driven by an insatiable need to uncover every detail of a story—and to know it before anyone else. It was more than just curiosity, it was a deep, burning urgency, especially because the story unfolded in America. How could something so monumental happen in a country with one of the world's top intelligence agencies and an unparalleled investment in security? It was surreal.

As the events unfolded, they resonated within me like a thunderclap, awakening a fervour I thought had dimmed. Each development pulled me back into the intricate world of foreign policy with an irresistible force, igniting a fire in my soul. I felt an undeniable personal connection, as if this unfolding narrative was not just a story but my own—one that demanded to be understood and shared.

In the wake of terrible tragedy, my love for journalism surged back to life, fuelled by this profound connection and an unyielding desire to dig deeper. I was driven by an insatiable thirst for knowledge, eager to be among the first to unravel the truth and illuminate the complexities of our world. This was more than just a profession; it was a calling, a passionate quest for understanding that I was ready to embrace with open arms.

A few months later, I became the news editor of the university's student paper, *The Back Hill Reporter*, a role that felt even heavier in the wake of such world-altering events. Leni was also a member of the editorial team. We covered the anti-war protests that surged in response to September 11, with hundreds of thousands taking to the streets of London. I was there, armed with my National Union of Journalists student press card, while Yuki, a keen photographer, captured the collective grief and outrage with her camera. I remember vividly an older American lady, tears streaming down her face, crying out at the protesters. Her voice, heavy with sorrow, called for retribution for her slain countrymen, but her cries were lost amidst the marching crowd. It's possible she didn't fully anticipate the complex ramifications of advocating for military intervention and its potential impact on America's global standing. Historically, the US has often relied on military solutions or providing aid to allies in conflicts, sometimes at the expense of other diplomatic avenues. As the geopolitical landscape evolved, there was an opportunity for America to adapt its foreign policy approach to better address the nuanced challenges of today's world. The international community had changed significantly, as had perspectives on conflict resolution, creating a need for diverse and multifaceted strategies in foreign affairs.

By Christmas 2001, Mama had become engaged to Frank. I remember the hilarious moment when he nervously told me he had proposed to Mama, almost as if he was seeking my permission. It was amusing to see him like that, reminding me of A.L. and his nerves when he first met Mama. I had no objections. Mama deserved happiness, and I had no reason to oppose the engagement. It felt like we were going to form a happy family. My relationship with Mama wouldn't change. I felt reassured knowing that if I moved elsewhere, she would have Frank by her side and wouldn't be alone. Frank always made me feel like I belonged to his family, not just as his wife's daughter. But I also knew that once they got married, we would move in with Frank. His house was much larger, and Mama wouldn't have it any other way, especially since Frank's daughter was also living with him.

Then, in the second quarter of 2002, more good news arrived: Mama and I became British citizens. It felt like a long-awaited victory, a moment of triumph after years of uncertainty. We no longer had to worry about our status in the UK, and we had a sense of safety and security and were also able to travel freely. Gone were the days of the baby blue travel document. We now held British citizenship and would soon apply for passports that granted us visa-free access to most of the world. This change brought a profound sense of belonging and security, a weight off our shoulders.

Around this time, however, we faced a sadder change. Our beloved neighbour, George, passed away. He was taken to the hospital one day by an ambulance and never returned home. Mama and I were both deeply saddened by his loss. George had been like a member of our extended family, always so gracious and kind. We had grown close over the years, and his absence left a void. His nephew visited us after his passing to express his gratitude for the care we had shown George. He knew about us because George often spoke of Mama's generosity and the meals she prepared for him.

Life was changing rapidly, with some changes bringing joy and others sorrow. The tragic events of September 11 were etched deeply in my mind. By the time I finished my studies and received my grade, I was well versed in the US foreign policy that was reshaping the world. In Britain, tension hung in the air as Prime Minister Tony Blair closely followed President George W. Bush's war decisions.

I graduated with a degree in Journalism. Frank and Mama attended the ceremony together, and Frank even posed with us for official photos. My father didn't attend, still harbouring a special dislike for Britain that kept him from setting foot in the country. But despite his absence, it was a proud moment, a culmination of years of hard work and perseverance.

Then just as I was beginning to map out my future, a call from CNN altered my path. It came right after one of my examiners, who was part of the British Press Complaints Commission, was heading to Bosnia to work on their version of the commission there. He had confessed to me during a phone call after my graduation that my dissertation was the best piece of work on Bosnia he had ever read. He said that it had finally helped him understand the complexities of the situation in the country, allowing him to undertake his task with newfound clarity. I was told it wasn't he who passed my thesis to CNN, and I never found out who did.

CNN wanted me to come in for an interview for an internship. I could hardly believe it. I had spent countless hours watching their coverage during the war in Bosnia and had been glued to the screen throughout the reporting of September 11. Now, I had the chance to be part of that very network. It was a dream come true although tinged with the sorrow of a world forever altered.

But amidst the heavy global changes, a beacon of joy shone through: Mama's and Frank's wedding. It was a lively affair, attended by my university friends, including S.W., Yuki, Tomoko, Leni, and her boyfriend who had all become like family. My former French teacher from Trinity School, Mary, and her husband Tim also attended. My brother didn't attend; he simply didn't want to. Looking back, I remember how my father's constant criticism of Mama had become like a broken record. Husein, being easily influenced, absorbed these negative sentiments and became almost like a puppet controlled by my father. Although my relationship with Husein didn't change, I found myself questioning his unwillingness to make an effort.

I wondered about his plans when Mama and Frank would visit Sarajevo. Did he intend to avoid them entirely? Or did he assume he could insist on seeing just Mama, or perhaps neither of them? His reasoning puzzled me deeply.

Despite my confusion and disappointment, I recognised that ultimately, it was his choice to make. I couldn't force him to change his stance, even if I disagreed with it. The situation left me feeling conflicted, caught between my love for my family members and the growing divide between them.

But during the reception, I delivered a speech in my best journalistic style, recounting the time I first met Frank and how nervous he was, but despite that, how he had always been good to Mama and made her happy. The celebration was full of joy. At one point, one of his lively relatives started a conga line, and S.W. laughed so hard that she ended up in a hilarious photo that looked like a university reunion, with me, Tomoko, and Yuki all in one shot in the conga line. In some ways, it reminded me of the roller-skate train I formed as a child in Bosnia before the war, a carefree moment in a world that had once been safe.

What really solidified the bond between Frank and Mama was their shared love of food, deeply rooted in both their cultures. He also understood the pain of losing a homeland and the anguish of watching it disintegrate. My maternal grandma, Sadika, had died in Czechoslovakia during the conflict that Frank deeply understood. He had fled Czechoslovakia in 1968 during the Prague Spring when Alexander Dubcek introduced reforms for "socialism with a human face," including freedom of speech, political liberalisation, economic reforms, and civic rights. On August 20–21, 1968, Warsaw Pact troops invaded, meeting widespread nonviolent resistance but quickly prevailing due to their military superiority. The Prague Spring ended on August 21, 1968, and is remembered as a significant but ultimately tragic attempt to reform communism under an authoritarian regime backed by external forces. Frank, like many others, had a background marked by political upheaval.

Frank loved Mama's Bosnian cooking and occasionally made Slovak dishes. He had three children: two sons older than me and a daughter close to my age. By the time Mama and Frank married, his daughter and I were living with them. I got along with Frank well and never had any issues with him. Mama was happy, and that was enough for me.

A BRUSH WITH THE MEDIA GIANTS

The day arrived for my visit to CNN's London bureau, a small ivory-colour building nestled between a restaurant and another office on Great Marlborough Street. I stepped through the revolving doors into a compact reception area adorned with numerous small television screens broadcasting various Turner Broadcasting channels, which owned CNN at the time. After I informed the receptionist of my appointment, she handed me a pass and asked me to wait. My excitement was palpable.

Soon, a tall, grey-haired man in a white shirt and jeans approached. P.T., an American just over six feet tall, greeted me with a handshake. As we exchanged pleasantries, he mentioned having read my dissertation. Surprised, I inquired how he obtained it. He vaguely mentioned it being sent to him but offered no further details. When I asked his thoughts on it, he praised it as the best academic work on Bosnia he had read. He revealed he had been a producer in Sarajevo during the war, his eyes momentarily reflecting the sorrow of those memories. He described it as the most brutal war he had witnessed.

We proceeded toward the offices, passing the newsroom I would see later. I sat facing P.T. and another producer while they questioned me about my university studies. What was supposed to be a fifteen-minute interview extended to forty-five minutes due to our engaging conversation. When asked why I wanted to intern at CNN, I explained my admiration for the channel since the Bosnian War. "I always aspired to be a war journalist like Christiane Amanpour, eager to tell the stories of those who needed their voices heard. But most of all, I want to know the news immediately as it happens. I don't want to work for a print newspaper where I have to wait till the next day to inform my reader, and even then, it would be old news because so much would happen overnight." P.T. nodded approvingly, a smile hinting at the corner of his mouth. I knew I had secured the internship.

When I told Mama the news, her face lit up with pure joy and pride. It was as if all those years of my obsession with CNN, every moment I had spent glued to the screen during the war in Bosnia and the events of 9/11, every essay I had poured my heart into, and all the relentless research for my dissertation had culminated in this one, extraordinary opportunity. She saw it as the moment when everything finally came together, the moment when all my hard work paid off. She knew how much this meant to me, and her happiness radiated through the room.

My father was pleased too, but his excitement couldn't match Mama's. She was over the moon, sharing in my elation as if this victory was her own. As for me, I was floating on air. Nothing and no one could have brought me down from that high. This was the era that was shaping the world, and I was going to be right in the middle of it.

I was to start in September after a graduation trip to Italy, a gift from Mama and one I relished. Just a couple of days after my interview, I jetted off to Rome, ready to dive into its rich tapestry of history. I had visited Italy several times before, primarily Milan where I had friends, using the baby blue travel document that allowed me to travel only within Schengen member states. However, this time was different. I was traveling as a British citizen with my British passport.

My friend and I were on a mission to explore every nook and cranny of the ancient city. We tackled the iconic slanted staircase and then ascended the spiral staircase that led us to the breathtaking dome of St. Peter's Basilica. Standing there, gazing out over the stunning St. Peter's Square, I felt like Rocky Balboa triumphantly reaching the top of those famous steps! It was not just about conquering stairs; it was a glorious celebration of my graduation and the thrilling internship that awaited me.

Even while I was in Rome, a city steeped in history and grandeur, my thoughts kept drifting to the moment I would walk through the doors of CNN and step into that newsroom. The anticipation was electric, coursing through me with every passing day. No other channel held the level of excitement, the sense of destiny, like CNN did. It was a dream that was now, finally, coming true.

Returning from Rome, I began my internship at CNN in late September 2002, stepping into the newsroom not as an interviewee but as an intern ready to dive into international news coverage. My desk was next to the news-gathering desk, and I embraced the varied shifts, relishing every moment. My dedication did not go unnoticed. After an early shift, the

American executive producer commended my spirit, hinting at a potential news assistant job.

Around this time, A.L. and I ended our relationship. Before Mama's wedding, he had returned to the US. I realised that long distance wasn't going to work for me. I quickly forgot about it all, as the excitement of CNN was better than anything else and I was young, there was going to be another boyfriend, this just wasn't the time.

Two weeks into my internship, Bosnia was preparing for its October general elections, and rumours of postal voting discrepancies emerged. My brother was working for the Organization for Security and Co-operation in Europe in Sarajevo and informed me of these issues. He did so because I was at CNN, and he wanted to give me a story to pitch. And I did. I pitched the story to the news desk, careful not to disclose my source. The executive producer asked me to write the story and secure an interview. I exceeded expectations by arranging an exclusive interview with Bosnia's High Representative, Lord Paddy Ashdown. The CNN team was impressed, and I was told to come in at six in the morning to see it live.

But one of the most unforgettable moments was encountering Christiane Amanpour in the hallway. Starstruck, I told her how much her reporting from Bosnia meant to us Bosnians. She was warm and down to earth, embodying the bravery and dedication of women journalists such as Samantha Power, Janine di Giovanni, Maggie O'Kane, and many others who reported from war zones. Amanpour was kind and we chatted for a bit. She asked where I was from in Bosnia, and she knew exactly where Brcko was. I had no doubt that she had traversed the entire country during the war. She was like a walking map of Bosnia.

In my final week, I sought a meeting with the bureau chief because of the news assistant job that was currently being advertised but instead met a senior English executive who was visiting from the US, where he was based. Presenting my case for the job, I was shocked when he dismissively told me I would never work in the UK media and should return to Bosnia. His words were a stark contrast to my positive experiences at CNN. It was the first time I would face that level of discrimination, and at the time I could not understand. When I gasped and responded, "Excuse me?" he responded, "You heard me." I then said, "Well, maybe not here, but you don't get to decide where I work." He had a disgusting smirk on his face, probably assuming he was better than me. He reminded me of those characters my father had interacted with and never had anything good to say about. He acted like he could do and say whatever he wanted. After all, he was in his country, and I was just some former refugee.

My time at CNN was a blend of exhilaration, learning, and unexpected challenges. Although I did not secure a permanent position, the newsroom experience solidified my passion for journalism and the resilience needed to pursue it more than ever.

THE LANGUAGE WE SPEAK

Less than a year had passed since my internship at CNN, and I was still job hunting without any success. Invitations for job interviews were non-existent, not even for internships. I was applying for any kind of entry level media role, including newspapers and broadcast networks, think tanks, PR firms. Meanwhile, all my university friends, both British and non-British, were advancing in their careers in London. Mine was at a standstill. I continued working at my old student job in a department store on weekends while job hunting during the week.

With so much time on my hands, Mama, Frank, his daughter, and I decided to take a trip to Slovenia, Croatia, Bosnia, and Slovakia by car. The ultimate road trip from the UK and back. It was Mama's and my first visit since we left in 1992. The sun's rays reminded me of the day we left Brcko, but this time, I was returning to my homeland. The strong Herzegovina sunshine I remembered from childhood welcomed me back. After years of living in the UK, I had acclimatised to northwestern European weather. It must have been 35°C—scorching, just like every summer before the war. The heat was relentless, with the sun high in a cloudless azure sky. The air was dry, only occasionally stirred by a faint, warm breeze. The intense heat radiated from the ground, making the asphalt feel almost sticky underfoot. The air shimmered with heatwaves, creating mirage-like effects on distant horizons.

Amid this sweltering scene, the rugged terrain of Herzegovina stood resilient. Olive trees, cypresses, and hardy Mediterranean shrubs dotted the landscape, their leaves glistening under the bright sunlight. The tall grasses and wildflowers swayed gently, their vibrant colours contrasting with the sun-bleached earth.

In towns and villages, whitewashed stone buildings with terracotta roofs reflected the harsh sunlight, creating a blinding glare. Narrow, winding streets were quiet as people sought refuge indoors from the scorching temperatures. Shutters were drawn, and the air outside felt almost deserted, save for the occasional song of cicadas.

Despite all the tranquil beauty, what struck me the most was the smoothness of the road, like the one we travelled on when we left Bosnia. Even the plants on both sides of the road were familiar: green tall grasses swaying in the soft breeze, just like every summer I remembered. The only difference now was that the war had ended, we were not being chased, and there were no paramilitaries and no makeshift borders. Instead, the peace was somewhat stable, maintained by the rocky Dayton Peace Agreement.

So here I was in Bill Clinton's version of peace. Under his administration, the war in Bosnia ended after extreme public pressure during his re-election campaign. Mama and I were back in a different version of our homeland, eleven years after we left as refugees. Under the Dayton Peace Agreement, Bosnia and Herzegovina was now divided along ethnic lines into two main entities. The Federation of Bosnia and Herzegovina, where Bosniaks and Bosnian Croats predominantly reside. The other entity, Republika Srpska, was formed from acts of genocide and where Bosnian Serbs are a majority.

But still, I was excited to be back. I had left as a child and returned as an adult. Years had passed in the safety of Britain while blood was spilt in the Bosnian War. I had been a refugee for half a decade but entered my homeland as a British citizen, free of labels. At least that's what I thought. I had longed to visit Bosnia to see how it had developed after the war had ruined its infrastructure and historic monuments that had stood for centuries. The opportunity only arose when we became British citizens. The travel document we had prior to citizenship meant we couldn't go to Bosnia because that document couldn't guarantee us safety if something happened to us. We were supposed to make this visit to Bosnia after my graduation, but my CNN internship was far more important than a road trip.

We stopped in the middle of nowhere, at a petrol station so small there was only one pump. I could not tell how far from the nearest big town we were, but there were only two other people in the shop with the old greying salesman with the round stomach I presumed owned this business. I needed batteries for my ancient camera because I had already taken too many photos and was worried I might not have enough juice in the camera to make it to Sarajevo. As per usual, I needed photographic evidence of every millimetre of that trip. I approached like a deer in headlights, aware that over the years my Bosnian language had faded away. Ninety-nine percent of everything I did was in English. I even began to dream in English. It was part of my life and one in which I could express myself better than I could in my mother tongue. I had left the Bosnian education system at the age of eleven, the day I became a refugee, and although I had gone to school in Zagreb, at that point, Croats had begun to change their language so that they could get away from calling it Serbo-Croat. So, standing in front of this man who not only spoke Bosnian but did so with a Herzegovina dialect posed a massive challenge for me. The words were not quite ready to leave my mouth; better yet, how would the words be formed? Directly translated from English? At that point it was my only option, but I had forgotten so many words that I did not even know what a translation would have resembled. We stood eyeing each other like we were about to enter a boxing ring. I wondered what he thought at that moment. He could not have mistaken me for a foreigner. Surely, I looked Bosnian. After a few minutes of eyeing each other, I decided the safest option was to get Mama and ask her to talk on my behalf, as I certainly would not do that myself.

Mama, sitting in the car, watched me walk back looking agitated and instantly knew the problem. But she pretended not to know. She asked me in simple Bosnian, which I could still understand, "Did you get the batteries?" and I responded in English, "I have never been more exhausted trying to buy batteries. Can you please get them for me?" I felt like I was sweating, not from the hot Bosnian summer but from the stress of trying to buy an item. Mama rolled her eyes and said, "OK, let's go."

We strolled into the shop, with Mama in front, fearless as ever, while I lagged behind, doing my best impression of a human-shape shadow blending into the shelves. If chameleons had an identity crisis, that was me. I'm taller than she, but somehow, I felt like a preschooler clinging to Mama's pant leg for dear life.

Mama flashed her megawatt smile at the store clerk, and they started chatting like two long-lost besties at a high school reunion. Then the guy leans in, dead serious, and asks, "So, are you her translator too?" Mama laughs. "Oh, you know how it goes with these young ones. They leave Bosnia for five minutes and suddenly forget every word!" The clerk nodded like he'd just discovered the meaning of life. "Oh, I know that feeling. Got a few in my family just like that." Great. Just what I needed, a front-row seat to my own roast.

But they were spot on! I was one of many Bosnians grappling with a language dilemma. It was astounding to see how some, even older than I, had completely lost touch with their mother tongue. For those born abroad, some never got the chance to learn it, whereas others were whisked off to special Bosnian language schools.

But here's the kicker: Studies have shown that long-term migrants and refugee children can lose their ability to speak their native language. In my case, as a refugee, the trauma of war triggered this linguistic loss. It's fascinating to learn that a person's language skills up to age twelve are particularly vulnerable to change, especially when uprooted from their birthplace. So, it was only natural that my Bosnian would start to slip away.

I had tucked my Bosnian language into a mental box, stashing it away like forgotten treasures in an attic. It sat there, collecting dust, with no plans for a comeback, until that moment in Herzegovina. That eye-opening experience at the petrol station jolted me into action, forcing me to reassess my relationship with my mother tongue.

From that point on, I was on a mission. I dove headfirst into Bosnian culture, buying movies and music as if my life depended on it. I belted out Bosnian tunes like I was headlining a rock concert. I pored over newspapers like an eager retiree at breakfast, constantly pestering Mama about unfamiliar words. And then, my father sent me a massive Bosnian–English dictionary, and that became my reference point too as I navigated this linguistic adventure.

My efforts to reclaim my native language weren't just a task but an exhilarating journey of self-discovery and cultural reconnection. It was as if I was unlocking a part of myself that had been dormant for years, and it felt incredible.

GHOSTS OF SARAJEVO

As we drove into Sarajevo, a wave of melancholy washed over me when I spotted the tall yellow building, now infamous from the 1,425 days of the Siege of Sarajevo. The Holiday Inn had once housed the world's media, who, alongside the city's residents, became targets for Serbian snipers perched on the surrounding hills. From April 5, 1992, to February 29, 1996, Sarajevo endured the longest siege of a capital city in the history of modern warfare. It was relentlessly bombarded. On average, 329 projectiles were fired at the city daily, and nearly 50,000 tons of artillery projectiles were fired in total. During the siege of Sarajevo, 120 mortars and 250 tanks of the JNA were stationed around the city alongside the Army of Republika Srpska, under the command of General Mladic, also known as the Butcher of Bosnia. During the siege of Sarajevo, over 11,000 people, including 1,600 children, were killed, and 50,000 people were wounded. General Mladic's goal was to terrorise, torture, and demoralise the population in the cruellest ways possible. Throughout the war, Sarajevo, just like the rest of Bosnia and Herzegovina, was left to bleed, its cries for help largely ignored by the West.

I stepped out of our car at a crossroads near the Holiday Inn, standing in a wide-open space devoid of cars. It felt as if I had been transported back to a time when the only people around were those running for their lives. The emptiness was reminiscent of some of the darkest days of the siege. In the present-day August heat, the streets were mostly deserted save for a few tourists. I stood close to the traffic light, wary of any unexpected vehicles. To my right were the hills where Serbian forces had once positioned themselves, and to my left, a wide road flanked by a mix of new businesses and old apartment buildings scarred by mortar shells and bullet holes. In front of me, a long road stretched past the hotel. I stood there, almost seeing the ghosts of Sarajevo's past, the people running from sniper fire, their ghosts running through me.

It felt like hours, though it had only been minutes. I was overwhelmed. Dressed in a spaghetti-strap top and linen trousers, I felt a breeze on my neck. My hair, gently swaying on my shoulders, moved to the side. I couldn't bring myself to move, as if something held me there, making me a witness to a tragedy long past but never forgotten. Sarajevo had a different soul now, but its tragedy mirrored the rest of Bosnia and Herzegovina. No other city bore the scars of the 1990s quite like this one. While Western leaders debated in comfort, the people of Bosnia died by the second. Bosnia was left to fend for itself. Yet the Army of Bosnia and Herzegovina fought heroically, their determination evident in the fact that Sarajevo never fell.

Taking a deep breath, I looked around one last time. I forced a smile and returned to the air-conditioned car. At a traffic light, an old tram stopped beside us. Inside, a middle-aged woman with bushy brown hair leaned her head against the window, her sad eyes meeting mine. The war's sorrow seemed to linger in her gaze. Our eyes met briefly before the tram moved on. Grief hung in the air, but it was most palpable in the eyes of the people.

We found a place to park near the National Theatre. My brother had decided to give Mama an ultimatum: He would meet with us, but he didn't want to meet Frank. How childish, I thought. A grown man to behave like that. Truly unbelievable. Frank didn't break our parents' marriage. Our father did that. Frank and Mama met years after our parents divorced. But Frank was fine with it, even if surprised. He and his daughter went for a walk, and Mama and I to meet Husein.

The heat was stifling, and only a few tourists braved it. After a few minutes of waiting, I saw him approaching. Husein had gained some weight. He wore glasses and seemed cheerful. He hugged Mama first, then me. The years that had passed suddenly felt both like a lifetime and just a moment when time seemed to stand still, and I felt an overwhelming sense of happiness but also sadness that it had been so long since I had seen him. He had changed. His hair was receding and no longer thick. The last time we saw him was when he and my father left London. It was August 2003 now. We took some pictures in front of the theatre, then went to a café where time flew by, and we nearly forgot we had to drive to Brcko that same day. We chatted as if no time had passed, switching between English and Bosnian. Husein's fluency helped bridge my gaps in Bosnian.

Husein's phone rang. It was our father, calling during his lunch break to say he could see me now. Mama chose to stay behind, enjoying a slice of her favourite cake while she waited for Frank to join her. She hadn't spoken to my father since their divorce in 1996 and didn't want to now. I promised her I wouldn't be long, knowing we had a journey ahead. My brother hugged Mama again, encouraging her to visit Sarajevo for a longer stay next time. We walked off, taking smaller streets lined with Austro-Hungarian architecture, remnants from when Bosnia was under their rule. Sarajevo was like a living history book, each corner revealing layers of its past under different empires.

Suddenly, I saw my father standing in the doorway of his workplace. He became emotional upon seeing me, hiding his face with his hands. It had been so long, yet he hadn't changed much. He still had thick black hair, glasses, and his usual summer attire of a light blue short-sleeved shirt and light-coloured trousers. He hugged me, asked about my journey, and then took me to a café across from his office. We chatted for about thirty minutes. He invited me to spend New Year's Eve with them, suggesting it would be cold but celebratory. I agreed, promising to look for flights. I was always up for an adventure, even if this one meant spending more time with my father in person. I hoped it might give us a chance to mend our relationship, at least to the point where we could be civil to each other, and where he would finally stop calling me names and blaming me for not moving to Bosnia with him. I was also excited about spending more time with my brother and meeting his friends. Plus, the idea of celebrating New Year's Eve in Bosnia again was appealing; there, it was a celebration like everyone's life depended on it.

We stood up, and he hugged me again. At six-one, I had to bend down to embrace him because he was only around five feet tall. I waved goodbye as he returned to his building. My brother then guided me through different streets, offering a mini tour. I loved being in Sarajevo, a city finally at peace, though its scars and memories would never fade.

I felt as though I had always been a part of this historic city, at least through my brother's eyes, who lived there after the war. In our many conversations, he would share stories and send photos about the rebuilding process, allowing me to see Sarajevo through his perspective. Most of our communication took place over email and Skype, and I believe this brought us closer together, as it was our only means of connection before my arrival in Bosnia. Despite the distance, he remained my brother, and we both worked to drown out our father's constant criticisms.

I often thought my brother had made a mistake by leaving London. I believed he should have stayed to finish his education and secure British citizenship for better opportunities. Yet, it was his decision to make, and although I sensed he regretted it, he never admitted it.

My excitement was tempered when it came to seeing my father. Yes, it was good to see him, but the years leading up to this meeting were fraught with feelings of betrayal. The way he left us—refusing to change the documents into Mama's name and then spending years belittling me—left scars that were hard to ignore. He treated me as if I had no right to forge my own path simply because I had refused to return with him. I felt a mix of emotions. It didn't evoke the same excitement as reuniting with my brother; instead, it was a complex blend of unresolved feelings that lingered in the air between us.

And when our meeting ended, Husein walked me back to where I could walk on my own to the car in which Mama and the others were waiting for me. We were headed to Brcko, leaving behind the bittersweet memories of Sarajevo.

ONCE AGAIN

Before the war, Brcko was the kind of place where everything seemed to come together. Nearly 90,000 people called it home, and it thrived as a melting pot of different cultures, ethnicities, and backgrounds. The town was like the heartbeat of the region, a crossroads where roads, railways, and rivers all met, connecting Bosnia to the rest of the world. But that same importance made it a prime target when the war broke out in 1992.

One of the key reasons Brcko became such a battleground was the Brcko Corridor, also called the Posavina Corridor. It was a narrow stretch of land, carved out by military force, running alongside the River Sava. This strip was the only way to keep the eastern and western parts of Republika Srpska connected. At its slimmest point, it was just four kilometres wide.

In April 1992, around the time my family and I left Brcko, everything changed. Serbian forces rolled into Brcko, along with paramilitary groups such as Arkan's Tigers and the White Eagles, and the violence came swiftly. They prepared kill lists with chilling precision, targeting anyone who wasn't Serbian, particularly members of non-Serbian political parties and educated Bosniaks. My father's friend warned my father that he and Mama were on one of those lists; this was on the same day my father picked up my cousin's car after Mama told him we needed to leave Brcko. My father was a particular target because he was a member of SDA and the local parliament, but being well educated, both my parents were the types targeted for killing. It was the beginning of atrocities that would scar the town for years to come.

Even after the war officially ended with the Dayton Peace Agreement in 1995, Brcko's fate remained uncertain. Its strategic value meant no easy solution could be found. It wasn't until 1999 that a decision was made. An international tribunal finally declared that Brcko would become its own district, a self-governing unit in Bosnia and Herzegovina. This decision was meant to protect the town's diverse character and help the people rebuild what had been shattered.

Officially established in 2000, the Brcko District became a condominium shared between Republika Srpska and the Federation of Bosnia and Herzegovina, while maintaining independent governance from both entities.

Now, eleven years later, in 2003, I stood on the edge of a new bridge overlooking the river. This border crossing once again directly connected Bosnia with Croatia. The river had transformed into a graveyard for genocide victims. To the left of the bridge stood a restaurant, eerily empty, perched on a structure resembling a chemical tanker. The emptiness was due to a combination of the early hour and the oppressive Bosnian heat. To the right lay the rest of the town. Ahead was a thick line of trees, the only thing that seemed unchanged since my childhood. They looked like a painting. As a child, I thought the bridge was endless, but as an adult, it felt like

I could cross it in no time at all, and we did. We crossed by car into Gunja, Croatia, to visit my Grandma Sadika's grave. Mama tenderly cleaned Grandma's grave, her hands gently brushing away the remnants of time, and placed fresh flowers with a loving touch. We lingered there, wrapped in our memories and shared sorrow, honouring her life in silence. It was a bittersweet moment; though our hearts ached, we took solace in knowing her resting place remained untouched by the ravages of war, a stark contrast to the devastation surrounding us in Brcko.

I had been away for so long. So much had changed. Brcko had transformed from a beautiful little town into a cold, ethnically divided district. As a child, I knew the city centre like the back of my hand, and that hadn't changed. But other parts of Brcko felt alien, unrecognisable. Mama had lived in Brcko her whole life, and for her, it was as though she had never left. So many places now housed different businesses, but there were also those dark spots used for the torture, rape, and murder of the non-Serb population during the 1990s wars.

We walked through the town, each place whispering a story. Some were notorious for their wartime horrors. For instance, what was once the Hotel Galeb is now the Hotel Jelena. That hotel was a notorious rape centre and brothel where Serbian soldiers held Bosniak women hostage, subjecting them to relentless rape and mental abuse. They were forced to work naked as waitresses, serving the men who were violating them. No one can ever truly grasp the fear and humiliation they endured. These systematic rapes shattered their mental health, social status, and subjected them to societal shame in a culture that has yet to address the rapes of the Bosnian War. The fact that this hotel still stands, even under a different name, and still hosts guests is abhorrent. I wondered who would even want to stay there. It should have been razed to the ground to erase any reminder of the war crimes committed against Bosniak women. Yet, no Western embassy or international body ever demanded its destruction. I cannot fathom how anyone could tolerate the existence of this notorious rape camp, let alone stay there.

We walked past businesses, most of them new, now occupying spaces where the old ones used to be. The newspaper shop where I used to buy all my Disney cartoon strips was now, I believe, a florist. Just a bit farther along, around the corner, was the city centre, a wide space surrounded by buildings in the Austro-Hungarian architectural style. In the middle stood a fountain of youth, a statue depicting two small children holding a fish as if steering it. Nearby was the building where my uncle's ex-girlfriend had lived. She was captured and systematically raped by Arkan's Tigers. They, along with other Serbian soldiers, kept her hostage in her apartment, never allowing her to lock the doors. They visited daily and at all times of the night, raping her repeatedly, sometimes one after the other. She became pregnant because of those attacks. When she wanted to abort, the Serbian rapists forced her to carry the pregnancy to full term. After she gave birth, they took the baby to Serbia. Eventually, she hanged herself.

Each place in Brcko bears the weight of war crimes committed there. Serbian soldiers would sometimes rape women in their homes, forcing their husbands, elderly parents, siblings, and children to watch in helpless anguish. The hospital, meant to be a place of healing, was also a site of these brutal acts. Such stories devastated Brcko during the 1990s war, and the passage of time has not healed its deep wounds. Some Serbs who committed these crimes and acts of genocide still roam freely in the divided city, and some are even members of Serbian political parties. Nikola Koljevic, my father's professor, was posthumously declared by the UN in 2016 to be part of a criminal enterprise with extreme views toward Bosniaks. My Bosnian Serb piano teacher became a war criminal. Everyone seemed to know someone involved in these atrocities, because their surviving victims refused to remain silent.

As we continued, we found ourselves in front of the Brcko police department, a notorious site where Bosniaks and other non-Serbs were tortured. This police station had become a concentration camp, a place of death and suffering. In front of it, a Humvee with a mounted machine gun was parked, occupied by three American soldiers. I stopped to chat with them. They were surprised to learn I was from Brcko. They were friendly, down-to-earth young men and we chatted and joked. After a few minutes, I asked for a photo, and they agreed. One of them climbed to assume a position next to the machine gun, and I loved it. In the picture, I looked like a journalist reporting from a war zone. We said goodbye to the soldiers, who waved and smiled warmly as we continued on our way. They remained in their vehicle, stationed in front of a place that should have protected civilians but instead tortured and killed them. I wondered how many war crime charges would have been handed to the Bosnian Serb police, Arkan's Tigers, police units from Serbia and Montenegro, and other Serbian forces if Western justice had been impartial to all religions, not just those deemed worthy by Western governments.

We continued our walk and arrived at Zelena Pijaca, an open-air fruit and vegetable market, a place I had visited with Mama countless times as a child. I remembered the fully ripe tomatoes and peppers, the beautifully arranged produce. Mama often bought peppers, potatoes, pod peas, apples, plums, and everything needed for traditional Bosnian savoury and sweet dishes. The market was like a magic farm, offering everything one could wish for in the kitchen. This time we visited out of curiosity. Though slightly changed, it still brimmed with produce from surrounding farms. I don't know how long it had remained closed when the war started, but I suppose it was only for a short period before being mainly run by Serbs untouched by Serbia's murderous regime. Some of these Serbs were not locals; they had moved to Brcko during the war, occupying the homes of those who had fled. Before these homes were occupied, Serb paramilitaries and local Serb neighbours looted them, stealing even window frames and toilet seats. I know because they stole such things from our apartment.

We moved on to another prewar memory, this time my old library in the building known as Brcko City Hall. As a child, I often visited it with my friends. The air always carried the scent of old book pages packed on shelves in a small, cozy space run by an elderly librarian. The library was housed in a building constructed during the Austro-Hungarian Empire, reflecting the architectural style of the last empire to rule over

Yugoslavia. Many of Brcko's buildings bore this influence. In contrast, the mosques were remnants of the Ottoman Empire, whose rule began when Mehmed the Conqueror invaded Bosnia in the fifteenth century. This period profoundly shaped Bosnia's religious and cultural identity. The mosques in Brcko stood as vivid testaments to Ottoman architecture.

Our final trip was to the Sava River, to the notorious Luka concentration camp. I wouldn't have gone in even if we were allowed. The Luka camp holds the darkest history of Brcko's war years. From May to June 1992, over 3,000 men and women were systematically murdered there. The camp housed another 1,000 civilians, 95 percent of whom were Bosniaks, the rest being Bosnian Croats. The killings were swift and brutal. Mass graves overflowed with victims, leading Serbs to burn bodies in kafilerija ovens once used for cattle.

The torture was unimaginably horrific. One man's ears were cut off with a knife. As he grabbed his head in agony, a female Serb assailant cut off his genitals. As he fell to the ground, he was shot in the head. Throughout May, detainees suffered similar fates: genitals cut off, eyes gouged, skin sliced to the bone. The brutality was unbearable. Special units from the Ministry of the Interior, or Specijalci, beat people with clubs and forced others to lick the blood from them. Chetniks, Yugoslav Federal Specijalci, and Serbian police were all involved in the torture, killing, and rapes. Women were raped in front of other detainees, especially their husbands. Girls as young as twelve were pinned down and violated in front of everyone. Members of non-Serb parties were captured, taken to Luka, and murdered within 24 hours.

Had we been caught, Mama, Tanja, and I would have been raped and possibly killed too. My brother and father would have been tortured and killed instantly. We would have been just more bodies in a mass grave.

The Luka concentration camp closed in July 1992, and the detainees were moved to their homes or other camps outside Brcko. My aunt was among those moved, imprisoned in her own home and my Uncle Huso to his.

The Brcko I had known and left was not the same town I returned to. It was not the beautiful place I remember as a child, when we were all united, when we didn't know the politics of division. Too much blood had been spilled and nothing has been learned from it. The West, as always, chooses to ignore that "Never Again" is meant to include all colours and religions, not a selective few.

PART IV (2005–2010)

A BRUSSELS CHRONICLE

The afternoon downpour in Brussels was unlike anything I had ever seen. It seemed as though the heavens had conspired to dump every drop of rain Europe had accumulated, all at once. I was caught in the throes of this deluge as I sprinted from Schuman Station to my apartment, a mere five minutes away. My umbrella, valiantly opened against the storm, surrendered almost immediately, collapsing under the weight of the rain. My shoulder-length hair, usually neatly styled, was plastered against my face, and water quickly seeped into my shoes, turning them into mini reservoirs.

By the time I reached my apartment building, I was thoroughly drenched. I fumbled for my keys in my handbag, the rain having made everything slippery and challenging. Entering the building felt like stepping out of a swimming pool fully dressed. Each step up the narrow staircase was accompanied by the squeak of my waterlogged shoes. I wasn't sure about removing them, not wanting my bare feet to touch the steps that countless others had trodden upon in their shoes. When I reached the third floor and unlocked my door, a wave of warmth embraced me.

It was March 2005, and I was navigating life in Brussels as a Blue Book stagiaire (intern) at the European Commission. I secured this coveted position after a strategic lunch meeting in December 2004 with a woman who worked in one of the Directorate Generals I had selected in my application as one of my three preferred options. A few days later, she informed me that I had made it to the stage, but I had to keep it under wraps until the official announcement. I had beaten the odds, becoming part of the elite one percent who gained this prestigious internship. What a tremendous relief! It felt far easier to gain experience abroad than it ever had in the UK. The mere thought of being part of the European Commission in Brussels was like the icing on a cake, filling me with excitement and possibility. I could almost envision myself walking through those historic halls, contributing to something meaningful and impactful. The opportunity felt like a dream come true, a chance to immerse myself in a vibrant culture while making a difference on a grand scale.

The pay was modest—around €400 or €500 a month, I think—which covered my rent and left a little for groceries. Social life, however, was far more appealing and inexpensive. I never turned on my TV during those six months because the vibrant social scene for stagiaires in Brussels offered far more excitement and engagement.

Leaving London was not a tough decision. Yes, I was going to miss Mama, but despite securing an internship with CNN, I had struggled to land a job in the UK. My stint at a department store, a holdover from my student days, had become increasingly frustrating. The offhand comment from the English CNN executive about me having no chance of getting a job there had only confirmed my growing dissatisfaction. When Leni, who had completed an internship the previous year, suggested I apply at the European Commission, I jumped at the chance. The opportunity to start afresh in Brussels was exactly what I needed.

But it was also fraught with sadness. Just the previous Christmas, Frank had been diagnosed with cancer on his second and third vertebrae. As a private patient, he underwent surgery in Harley Street, but due to the position of the tumour, they couldn't remove it.

He was then transferred to Kings College Hospital, marking the beginning of a long and challenging journey filled with surgeries. This news weighed heavily on our hearts, especially on Mama's. But even she wanted me to go to Brussels to have an opportunity that she hoped would lead to something new.

Within a month of moving to Brussels, I felt like a seasoned local. My apartment, located in the Schuman area in the European Quarter, was just minutes away from my workplace. The European Quarter, home to the iconic Berlaymont building, became my daily backdrop. Lunchtimes were spent with colleagues and friends, and my social circle quickly expanded beyond my DG for Internal Market.

I threw myself into my work at the Commission, taking pride in my role. My laid-back boss had taken paternity leave, leaving me with additional responsibilities. The head of my unit, an Irishman named Tony, gave me the freedom to work without breathing down my neck, and I managed press reviews, wrote articles for the Commission's magazine, and attended press conferences. Naturally, every meeting was conducted in French, and although I managed to catch a few words here and there, I spent most of my time battling the urge to snooze. Working in multiple EU languages, I rapidly picked up key terms and phrases, though I was by no means proficient. I remember a phone call from a German Commissioner's office, when the assistant inquired about the absence of German newspapers in my press review. The truth was I worked with what I was given. Unable to respond in German, I resorted to a tactic from a movie, loudly pretending the line was unclear and asking for an email instead. When the email arrived, I sought help from Carmen, my next-door neighbour and a translator in the DG translation unit.

Carmen, a petite Spaniard with a pixie haircut, was one of my favourite people in Brussels. Through her, I met many other Spanish stagiaires and attended Spanish-themed events. I bonded with other Spaniards over our French classes. Our weekends were filled with parties, and our group grew to include friends from across Europe and the Middle East, each bringing their own flavour to our vibrant social scene.

Once, reluctantly, I had to travel to Bosnia for five days. I was about as thrilled as a cat in a bath. With only six months in Brussels, I felt it was best not to waste valuable time on a trip to Bosnia when I could visit later. The opportunity to immerse myself in this vibrant city was too precious to pass up, and I wanted to make the most of every moment. The only thing that kept me going was the thought of getting back to Brussels, which felt like paradise compared to the Balkans. I had to swing by Sarajevo to sign some documents, and obviously, I crashed at my father's and brother's place.

My father was in utter shock at my nonstop party marathon, whereas my brother, upon hearing I had partied for two days straight without a wink of sleep, just looked at me and asked, "How are you still a functional human being?"

On the return trip from Sarajevo, I found myself in a taxi with a Belgian driver who was as cheery as a funeral director. This guy had a major bone to pick with the European Commission staff, claiming they were overpaid and that their stagiaires were basically a pack of wild party animals. He ranted and raved about how we were a menace to society.

"What do you do for a living?" he finally asked, and I thought, Oh no, not the dreaded question! I had two choices: Fess up and risk being thrown out of the taxi and made to walk back, or come up with a cunning lie. I decided to go with the safer option in case he spoke the same language. "Actually," I said with as much confidence as I could muster, "I'm part of the Croatian representation in Brussels." I knew they were there, although I had no clue if Bosnians were too, and I was basically making it up as I went along, but desperate times call for desperate measures. "And I totally agree with you! Those stagiaires—they're a real menace!"

The driver, seemingly mollified by my apparent solidarity, pressed for more details about my work. I was suddenly thrust into a verbal improvisation class, drawing from my memory of my Croatian friend David's endless stories about his previous work. I cobbled together a response with such passion and fervour that I half-believed my own bluff.

In the end, the driver seemed satisfied, and I made it back to Brussels without having to walk. The magic of improvising kept me from a very awkward, very long walk home!

One of the highlights of my time in Brussels was working on a political conference about the Western Balkans and EU enlargement. The team included David, a shy yet humorous Croat who became one of my closest friends alongside Nuala, a tall Dane. She was as tall as I, prompting David to refer to us as the Twin Towers. We spent a lot of time partying together or eating lunch during work week breaks at Berlaymont. Rafael, a tall Spaniard on a temporary assignment with the Commission, joined us as well. Rafael, Nuala, and David quickly became my favourite conference companions, all sharing a deep interest in the Balkans and a similar sense of humour. After I gave an interview to the Commission's magazine about the conference, my boss Tony ensured it was featured prominently in the press review and the DG's internal website.

During the planning stages, we decided not to invite a speaker from Montenegro, because the country was still part of Serbia at that time. A Montenegrin politician complained bitterly about this omission, despite our explanations. After considerable discussion and advice from DG Enlargement, we allowed her to represent Montenegro, albeit in a different manner from the other speakers. The conference, held in June 2005, was a resounding success. Our team, consisting of individuals from various former Yugoslav countries, managed to work together without ethnic tensions. We shared meals and laughter while we prepared for that event, and most of us remained good friends afterwards. I felt a deep sense of pride and enjoyment being among people who were once my fellow countrymen when Yugoslavia was still united. We didn't see each other through ethnic lenses but through the bonds of growing friendship, filled with the typical humour shared by our nations. I hoped the same spirit could grow among our other countrymen and women.

David and I were very good friends. He was charming and funny, and it was so easy to be his friend. One day, he called me at my office to inform me about a Finnish guy who was searching for me. This Finnish individual, a fan of Bosnian culture and food but a vegetarian, had heard about a Bosnian on the stage. Yes, me. He eventually found me, and soon we became friends. I organised a sirnica (Bosnian cheese pie) party at David's spacious apartment. The party was a hit, featuring guests from various countries and a generous supply of Bosnian plum brandy, rakija, which I avoided like the plague.

The Finnish friend soon became a regular at our gatherings. Our next party took place in Bruges, where David's connections at the College of Europe allowed us access. My old BTEC friend S.W. was visiting me and joined us on an afternoon sightseeing before heading to party. A shot of rakija seemed like a ritual at the entrance. I declined, as did S.W., only to be met with playful mockery from my friends. "What kind of Bosnian are you?" was the question. "The smart kind," was the answer. Rakija smelled like every booze-loving ghost from history decided to throw a party in a single bottle, and I'm pretty sure the taste was just as spirited! Later, when my sore throat worsened, I reluctantly used rakija diluted with water as a gargle in the bathroom, drawing amused stares from anyone who saw my unorthodox self-medication, which worked for a bit. Back in the old Yugoslavia, if a child had a fever, they'd soak their socks in rakija, slap them on the kid's feet, top it off with some dry socks, and then wrap the child in a duvet. By morning, the fever would have magically disappeared—the smell of those feet, not so much. So, I figured a little gargling with rakija might do wonders for my throat too, though I opted to skip the sock part.

As the night progressed, a Russian friend offered S.W. and me a ride back to Brussels. The trip was a real sardine can—four of us girls crammed into the back seat, three more up front, and the Russian and Czech who took up residence in the boot. We did cut them some slack, though. We took off the cover so they could poke their heads through like curious puppies. Despite the discomfort, we made it back to Brussels, and the Czech driver navigated safely. But as we rolled into Brussels and hit a traffic light, we were greeted by what seemed to be the only other car in the entire city. The occupants were practically hanging out their windows, pointing and laughing like they'd just seen a circus parade. And who could blame them? We looked like a family of clowns in a car. S.W. and I laughed at the sight of this, saying that the only thing this packed was the London Underground. No wonder then that the Russian and the other Czech struggled to stand after being cooped up for just over an hour in the boot of the car.

At around 3 a.m., after expressing my gratitude and ensuring the Russian and the Czechs were safely on their way, I fell into an exhausted sleep. But my rest was interrupted at 6 a.m. by a call from David, who was still in Bruges. He inquired about my whereabouts, and I explained that I had returned to Brussels with the Russians and the Czechs, reminding him that I had let him know and I had asked him to join. He did remember, though barely. David was in search of the Finn, and after some minutes I managed to track down their whereabouts and ensure they got back to Brussels safely. Despite my hoarse voice and exhaustion, we all reconvened in Brussels for dinner.

There was never a dull moment with my lively group of friends. However, the fun and laughter were overshadowed by a voice message from Mama a few days later. While attending a press conference, I received an incomplete message from her saying, "It is absolute devastation here," before the line cut off. I was anxious and immediately attempted to call her back, but the call wasn't getting through.

Returning to my office, I found a message from Tony to come and see him. In his office, his calm demeanour did little to ease my anxiety as he informed me of a terrorist attack in London. The attack had targeted buses and the Underground, and phone lines were suspended. My heart sank as I learned that I couldn't reach Mama. I asked Tony about his daughters, and he said thankfully they were not in London.

I returned to my desk, unable to focus on work. The news of the attack, combined with my personal connection to London, left me feeling hollow. It must have been sometime in the afternoon when I finally managed to reach Mama on the phone from my office. When she answered, a wave of relief washed over me. Hearing her voice brought comfort as she assured me that she was home and that everyone was safe. During this time, Frank had recovered from cancer and returned home, so Mama and he were at least enjoying their life and working, but not traveling much to central London.

After our conversation, I reached out to Leni, S.W., and all my other friends. Each call eased my worries further; knowing that everyone was safe felt like a heavy weight lifting off my shoulders. In that moment, I felt a deep sense of gratitude for their well-being and the connections we shared. But reflecting on the violence and loss, I realised how fortunate I had been to escape the attack but mourned for the lives that were lost.

In three weeks, I would have to return to London as my time at the Commission was coming to an end. I dreaded going back, not wanting to leave the vibrant life I had built in Brussels. My time there had been transformative, filled with friendships, laughter, and professional growth. The six months had felt like one long celebration, blending work with socialising, and I had formed lasting bonds with people from all corners of the globe. I knew then, there would be a lot of countries to visit. I was particularly excited about the prospect of seeing Jordan, where I envisioned myself hopping on a horse in Petra and unleashing my inner Indiana Jones. I could practically hear my friend Lana, with her unstoppable Jordanian zest, in the background yelling, "Indyyyyyyyy!" like she was auditioning for a role as my personal hype squad.

On my last day in Brussels, Tony and his team threw a surprise farewell party for me. They gifted me a Longchamp Le Pliage bag in olive green, a gesture that deepened my appreciation for both the brand and my unit. Tony was the best boss anyone could have, and I would miss the unit immensely.

As I packed my bags and readied myself to leave, the Eurostar transformed into my personal chariot, carrying not just my belongings but the vibrant spirit of Brussels that had woven itself into my very being. My time there had been nothing short of life changing. I longed for just a few more days, a few more moments to soak in the rich tapestry of cultures and friendships that filled my heart and soul.

Brussels, with its intimate size, pulsed with a social energy that made every encounter feel significant. I felt more alive there than I had in years, far surpassing the muted existence I experienced in London before 2005. Here, I could shed the weight of the barriers that had held me back, especially the relentless job hunt that had plagued my thoughts. Brussels opened my eyes to new dreams and aspirations, and in its embrace, I forged connections that would last a lifetime. This city was not just a chapter in my story, it was a catalyst for a vibrant, unbounded life.

THE DISPLACED DREAM

A month had passed since I left Brussels and returned to London, and it had been tough. The adjustment to London's vast size, its social scene, and the logistical challenges of getting from one place to another were overwhelming. The compact efficiency of Brussels had spoiled me, and I missed that city deeply. I joked to my Brussels friends that I was in mourning. It felt as though I had been abruptly yanked from a dreamlike existence—an enriching job and a vibrant social circle—and cast into the indifferent reality of post-Brussels London.

The most glaring issue, however, was my professional life. Whereas many of my fellow stagiaires who returned or moved to London seamlessly landed jobs, I found myself stuck in a frustrating cycle of endless applications and rejections. The job market seemed to close its doors to me.

Determined not to let my Brussels experience go to waste, I decided to apply for the British Civil Service Fast Stream, an accelerated development program aimed at cultivating future leaders within the government. Given my time at the European Commission, I thought my background in international affairs and my unique perspective as an ethnic minority made me an ideal candidate. My friends, recognising my qualifications and the strength of my application, encouraged me to apply.

The application process was straightforward, and I was soon sitting an online test. The Civil Service test wasn't related to the actual duties of the job. The questions focused more on interpersonal dynamics and hypothetical workplace scenarios rather than any specific skills required for a government role. Unlike the European Commission's rigorous exams, which we stagiaires jokingly said required knowledge down to the name of the Commission's President José Manuel Barroso's dog, the Civil Service tests seemed designed for a different kind of candidate—one who was perhaps less accustomed to real-world pressures.

There were two components to the test: a mathematical section and a written one. The scenarios mostly involved resolving disputes or managing workload issues, situations I was used to handling during my time at the Commission. But this test seemed like it was written for someone who had never encountered such situations. My Brussels experience, where I routinely managed additional responsibilities without complaint, made me find the tests somewhat trivial. Nevertheless, I passed them and anticipated moving forward in the process.

To my surprise, passing the tests did not guarantee a job offer. I received a rejection shortly after, which bewildered me. I asked other applicants about their experiences; some who had failed parts of the test had still received offers. The lack of clear feedback from the Civil Service only added to my frustration. It seemed as if my success was being penalised rather than rewarded.

Feeling disheartened, I Skyped with my father. He asked how the job search was going, and I explained my situation and the frustration of not finding a job despite my efforts. My father, who had always been a complex figure in my life, listened with a look of restrained disapproval.

He launched into his usual rant about the English and their politics, as if I cared about his bitterness or personal grievances in that moment. None of it was meant to support me. It never was. It was always about him and his emotions.

But for me, it triggered a memory. Back when I was at CNN, I was told I'd never work in the UK. At the time, I thought they meant just in the media. Surely, they didn't mean in government too. The realisation hit me like a thunderbolt, sudden and jarring. Anger and frustration bubbled up inside me as my father stubbornly clung to his narrative, refusing to see beyond his own perspective. His warnings about my aspirations felt like a slap in the face, dismissing my choices and dreams with a wave of his hand. The gulf between us widened, his paranoia and bitterness clashing with my desire for independence and understanding.

I had always sensed there was so much more he wanted to share, yet he kept it locked away. It felt as if he was deliberately holding back, teasing me with fragments of his thoughts while pulling me along for his own amusement. The silence hung heavy between us, charged with unspoken words.

I had assumed that other sectors in London would be more open, but my continued lack of success suggested otherwise. I applied for postgraduate programs, hoping to improve my prospects. I was accepted into American University in Washington, DC, but the uncertainty of securing a full two-year scholarship made me turn down the offer. The cost was eyewatering at around $90,000 for tuition, accommodation, and other things, and nothing guaranteed that I would secure a scholarship. It was such a blow. I was desperate to get out and have a fresh start.

⚜

About a year later, I was journeying back to Zagreb, a city I hadn't visited since my departure in 1993. This return felt monumental, almost like a homecoming, because I was reuniting with friends from Brussels: David, Nuala, and others from our lively stagiaire days. The air was thick with nostalgia and excitement, and experiencing the city as an adult added a new layer of meaning to the trip.

I arrived first and made my way to David's place. That evening, we went out with some of his friends, and it struck me how different it felt to be there as an adult. We engaged in conversations and shared laughter reminiscent of our time in Brussels. Zagreb felt like another home I had left behind, and I was happy to be back.

Our forty-eight hours in Zagreb became a whirlwind of laughter and reconnection. After this enchanting interlude, we travelled to Rijeka, David's hometown, where we spent a day exploring the city. The next stop was one of Croatia's beautiful islands for a vacation, where the stunning landscape perfectly mirrored our exuberance. It culminated in a delightful birthday dinner organised for me by David and Nuala, which felt like a beautiful sequel to our lives—Stage 2.0—where the past seamlessly mingled with the present.

The town was alive with energy, its warm summer nights filled with sounds of joy and shared memories.

Before flying out from Zagreb, David and I took a nostalgic tour of the city. We visited the zoo, a place I had cherished as a child, and wandered through the historic parts of the city, navigating the hills that felt both familiar and refreshing. The sights stirred up lively memories, deepening my appreciation for the city.

By the time I returned to London, I felt invigorated, a renewed sense of purpose driving me. I was determined to maintain a positive outlook and focus on landing a job. That was all I wanted: a job that would pave the way for my next chapter.

WE MEET AGAIN

Five months after abandoning all hope of pursuing postgraduate education in the United States, I was in Germany in 2006. I was on a master's program for one year: European Studies. Luckily, it was all taught in English. As part of the course, I was set to join a class trip that would take us through Berlin, Brussels (where I would see David and Nuala), Luxembourg, and Strasbourg. The prospect of visiting Berlin filled me with anticipation, not merely because of its historical and cultural allure, but because it meant I would see my cousin Tanja and finally reconnect with my Aunt Rahima. She had moved to Berlin around 1994, escaping the horrors of the Bosnian genocide with the help of a Serbian friend who provided her with a false identity. She travelled through Serbia and Slovenia to reach safety.

Upon arriving in Berlin, I called Tanja to arrange to meet. Tanja and I had always been close but lost touch briefly after she moved to Berlin. But now as I studied in Germany, we stayed in touch, our bond a steady reference point amidst all the newness. Tanja and I might not have spoken as frequently as I did with my brother, but our connection endured.

My class schedule included visits to the Bundestag and the Memorial to the Murdered Jews of Europe, also known as the Holocaust Memorial. The visit to the memorial that day was particularly poignant. The silence on the cold Berlin day seemed almost palpable, amplifying the memorial's significance. The site, though devoid of buried bodies, was a powerful reminder of the atrocities committed. Standing there, I couldn't help but reflect on the parallel suffering of Bosnians during the 1990s. The crimes committed against us were eerily similar to those of the Holocaust, but without the meticulous record-keeping of the Nazis. The memorial's presence raised questions about when Europe might acknowledge Bosnia's suffering with a similar monument. The failure to intervene during the Bosnian War was a painful reminder of Europe's inaction.

As I mulled this over, I realised that Europe's stance was unlikely to change. I needed to clear my mind, so I made my way to meet Tanja. The last time I had seen her was in 1993, when she left Zagreb for Berlin. When I emerged from the station, I spotted her standing with her daughter. Over the fourteen years since our last meeting, Tanja had changed significantly. Her once wild curls were now tamed, and she had gained weight and aged. Her daughter resembled a younger version of her mother.

We recognised each other from a distance, and as I approached, our smiles grew wider. I was smiling so brightly, but I didn't really know how I felt inside. It had been such a long time since we'd last met, and we were both completely different people now. We embraced in a tight hug, and as we pulled away, we continued to smile. Tanja asked how I was and inquired if my journey to meet her had been smooth. She introduced me to her six-year-old daughter, who initially hid behind Tanja. After a few moments of coaxing, the little girl shyly greeted me. When we began to walk, she took my hand in a quiet gesture that felt like unspoken approval—perhaps trust, or even a hint of affection—while Tanja and I caught up.

The apartment was just around the corner, where I would also meet Tanja's husband and Aunt Rahima. Seeing my aunt caused a tightness in my chest. She stood up to greet me, and as I embraced her, tears welled up in my eyes. Though she looked well groomed, her eyes and the lines on her face told a different story. Her gaze was filled with a lingering fear, a stark reminder of the trauma she had endured. The years in Brcko had left her emotionally and physically scarred, yet there was a delicate grace about her.

Her first words to me were, "Oh my dear Nadina, you are so beautiful." I thanked her, returning the compliment. This exchange, though conventional, was imbued with deeper meaning. Tanja then introduced me to her husband, a German who did not speak Bosnian. I tried my best to communicate with him in German. He was a friendly and straightforward man, though significantly older than Tanja, a fact that my aunt found challenging.

We spent a few hours together before I had to leave to return to my class. My aunt was eager to hear about Mama, who was in London caring for Frank, who was battling cancer again. Aunt Rahima seemed genuinely concerned about it. The two women had been close before my parents' divorce, and our conversation was intimate, as if Tanja and her family were not even present. Reconnecting with my aunt after so many years of sorrow felt like a new beginning for our family. It was refreshing to talk to her as an adult. She inquired if I had a boyfriend in Germany, a typical question from Bosnian relatives. I told her about a German guy I had been seeing from the same university, but it had ended by that point. Excited, she asked, "Was he marriage material?" Ah, the classic question from elder Bosnians! It's as if having a boyfriend was some kind of sin that required a quick baptism through marriage. I confronted her with the shocking truth: His Croatian friend had convinced him that all Bosnians were historically Muslims. Because of this twisted belief, he decided he couldn't date me simply because I was a Muslim. My aunt looked confused, but recognised how much Germany has changed since the war in Bosnia. I nodded in agreement, pointing out that since September 11, all Western countries had undergone significant transformations.

I would have loved to have spent the entire evening with them, but my class commitments required my attention. Tanja kindly offered to drop me off because Berlin was unfamiliar to me, especially at night. I felt more comfortable having someone guide me rather than navigating the city on my own. Aunt Rahima wouldn't have let me go alone anyway. To maximize our time together, everyone, including her, joined us for the car ride. I remarked that the last time I had been in a packed car with Tanja was when we left Brcko in 1992. Tanja laughed, asking if I remembered it. I replied, "Every detail is etched in my memory."

While we drove, Tanja attempted to be a tour guide, but my aunt was more focused on talking with me. It became a chaotic family conversation with everyone speaking simultaneously. We finally arrived at my destination, and after hugging me, we parted with plans to meet again the following evening.

The next day arrived quickly. After more visits to German government buildings and seeing the remnants of the Berlin Wall, I headed to dinner with Tanja and Aunt Rahima who was dressed impeccably, maintaining the style she had always had in Brcko. We ordered dinner and spent the evening talking. I chose not to broach the subject of her ordeal in Bosnia during this joyful occasion. However, she did share some details, though nothing too graphic. I recounted a heated argument I had with a nationalist Serb classmate, which escalated when he questioned a Turkish visiting professor about the war's origins. The professor's shock and response that the Serbs were responsible led to a heated exchange. Aunt Rahima listened intently, her concern evident.

When I mentioned that the argument had reached a point where the professor jokingly suggested we needed UN peacekeepers, Aunt Rahima's reaction was serious and tinged with fear. "Don't argue with them," she warned. "They will hurt you." My heart ached for her, realising how deeply her trauma still affected her. It was as if she was still trapped in her past. Despite this, we continued to joke and reminisce about our time in Brcko. For a while, it felt as though we had returned to our hometown before the war.

As the restaurant began to close, we reluctantly prepared to part ways. I had no idea when I would see Aunt Rahima again. Just before leaving, she handed me some money, which I initially declined. She insisted, saying, "As a student, you must take it. Tanja was a university student too once, so I know how much it is needed." After a few moments of insistence, I accepted the money, touched by her gesture. It reminded me of the pocket money my brother and I used to receive from Aunt Rahima and Uncle Huso during our childhood, despite our parents also giving us pocket money.

We hugged and said our goodbyes. The next time I saw my aunt, she would barely recognise me.

BULLETS FROM
THE HILLS

After completing my studies in Germany, I returned to London brimming with hope and enthusiasm. Luck was on my side, and I landed a three-month internship at CNBC in London. The opportunity arose after a successful interview with the Head of News, an Iranian British journalist who was impressed by my diverse background and decided to offer me the position. Before starting, there was the customary procedure of a resume security check, which would take about a month to complete. With a bit of free time on my hands, I decided to visit my brother and father in Bosnia. I didn't want to be the one in the family holding a grudge, and after two years had passed since being turned down for the Civil Service job—and now post-Germany—I thought maybe my father would understand me a bit better. It was my brother who insisted I come for a visit, saying it would be a vacation before the CNBC whirlwind hit. I always enjoyed visiting Bosnia and my brother, despite the fact that girlfriends and wives of his friends—who were only a couple of years older than me—acted like old aunts, bombarding me with questions about my love life and when I planned to tie the knot. It was relentless!

My father was no different. He decided it was time to find me a husband without even asking if I was okay with that. He invited a friend to bring her son to coffee with us at a restaurant overlooking Sarajevo. At that time, I was dating an Englishman and had no interest in being a means for his friend's son to escape the struggling economy in Bosnia. My father, however, didn't care, especially since I was with someone from a nation he despised. He judged every Englishman based on the politics of the Foreign Office, even though that perspective was completely misguided. It was a desperate attempt by him and his friend to completely ignore my wishes while trying to push her son onto me, and neither of them was impressed by my lack of interest. When we got back to his apartment, I made it clear that I was unavailable and that he should never attempt something like that again without consulting me first. The thought of him trying to orchestrate my personal life horrified me, especially since he had hardly been involved in my life since leaving London. At one point, he said, "But you'd be doing my friend a favour by helping her son." I shot back, "So my happiness doesn't matter as long as her lazy son feels good about himself for winning a passport lottery? Not a chance." It was clear that my happiness didn't concern my father, as long as he could impress his friend.

My always complicated relationship with my father was made even more so by his own egotistical behaviour. His stubbornness was a defining trait. He saw things solely from his perspective, as if his views were the gospel truth. His articles, in his eyes, were sacred scrolls that boosted his ego and inflated his self-importance. He operated like an authoritarian leader, where his opinions were paramount, and everything had to revolve around him. Acknowledging or valuing others' contributions was not in his playbook.

Despite the occasional family drama, I absolutely loved my visits to Sarajevo. I had a good relationship with my brother, and we had spent a lot of time travelling Bosnia up and down. But I was also good friends with some of his friends, so there was never a dull moment.

No matter what we were doing, my brother and I always had a blast. I still chuckle about the time we were on top of Mount Bjelasnica, sipping coffee with his friends. As we got ready for a group photo, someone accidentally knocked over a coffee cup, creating an epic coffee waterfall. The others were in a state of shock, but I just kept my cool and smiled for the camera. This little mishap quickly became the favourite joke; apparently, I had a superpower for staying unflappable.

We also enjoyed day trips in the scorching Bosnian heat. Sometimes to Mostar and surrounding areas and other times to Brcko when my father needed some documents. Spending time with Husein was a joy. He always had amusing stories or interesting titbits to share, and I would often tell him about my experiences in Brussels and London. I knew about every girl he dated and sometimes offered him advice on our usual Skype calls.

One August morning, my brother had to head to work, so my father suggested we take an early drive. The air was sticky as the sun began to rise over the hills, casting a warm golden glow on Sarajevo. The temperature was about 20°C and gradually warming up as the day progressed. As we drove through Sarajevo's city centre, the scent of freshly baked bread and strong Bosnian coffee filled the air, wafting through the narrow streets and alleyways of the old town, Bascarsija. Street vendors were setting up their stalls, displaying colourful fruits, vegetables, and handmade crafts. The call to prayer from the Gazi Husrev-beg Mosque echoed softly, blending with the sounds of the city waking up. Locals and tourists began to fill the cobblestone streets, some heading to work, others strolling leisurely, soaking in the rich history and vibrant culture. Outdoor cafés started to bustle with patrons enjoying their morning coffee and pastries. The morning light highlighted Sarajevo's blend of Ottoman, Austro-Hungarian, and modern architecture, creating a stunning backdrop for the day's activities.

As we drove toward the outskirts of the city, the urban landscape gradually gave way to quieter neighbourhoods and residential areas. The sounds of the city diminished, replaced by the chirping of birds and the rustling of leaves. The roads began to wind and climb, leading us higher into the hills. The ascent offered increasingly breathtaking views of Sarajevo below, with its iconic red-roofed buildings and minarets now appearing as miniature structures in the distance. The air grew cooler and fresher, filled with the scent of pine and wildflowers. The city's noise faded into the background, replaced by the peaceful silence of nature.

We passed by small houses where life moved at a slower pace. Traditional homes with terracotta roofs dotted the landscape, and locals tended their gardens while children played outside. Reaching the higher elevations, we found ourselves surrounded by serene landscapes, far removed from the hustle and bustle of the city. The air was crisp, the tranquillity almost palpable. Here, we could explore hiking trails, peaceful meadows, and scenic viewpoints offering stunning perspectives of the city below.

When we finally arrived at our destination, I stepped out of the car to take in the view of the city below. The air was cooler up here, and the cloud that had blanketed the city had cleared away. Looking around at the surrounding hills, I was reminded of their significance. To tourists, they might appear as beautiful landscapes of pristine nature, but to me, they were the very places from which Serbian snipers targeted Bosnian civilians during the siege of Sarajevo. These were the hills from which civilians were shot at in the city below and where children had been targeted as if they were mere game for war criminals.

A glance at the now-peaceful city revealed historic attractions such as a mosque, a church, and a synagogue, all situated close to one another, reflecting the harmony that had once existed among their worshippers before the war. Scattered around the city were cemeteries, many of which had been created during the conflict.

That morning on the hill, my father treated his cigarette with the meticulous care of someone defusing a bomb. He placed it in his pipe, and said, "*Ljiljan.*" I could tell exactly where this was going. "I had to leave the UK," he said, sounding like he was the one wronged.

My father had frequently expressed his disdain for the UK, accusing it of complicity in the genocide in Bosnia. He had a particular grievance with Douglas Hurd, the UK's Conservative Foreign Affairs Minister during the war years, whom he blamed for his role in the UN's arms embargo on

Bosnia. My father's outrage was well founded. The UK had been a significant force behind the arms embargo, which severely restricted Bosnia's ability to defend itself. During the Clinton administration, the late Republican Senator Bob Dole had identified Britain as the greatest obstacle to lifting the embargo. Each time the US pushed for it, Hurd intervened, arguing that lifting it would only lead to more deaths, and yet grave after grave was filled with Bosnianks.[17]

When my father first arrived in the UK as an exchange student in the 1960s, his youthful idealism must have been in overdrive. He envisioned Britain as the land of progressive political views and social justice. This idealism persisted even when he was studying English literature at the University of Sarajevo. He and Mama had hoped to send my brother and me to university in the UK, anticipating we would benefit from a Western education. But as the political climate soured, the disillusionment grew, prompting us to relocate to the UK as refugees.

When we arrived in the UK, my parents immersed themselves in political activism to defend Bosnia. They were like shocked tourists witnessing their vacation spot's worst side. Mama was angry with British foreign policy but, ever the pragmatist, wasn't keen on moving back to a war-torn country. But my father couldn't cope, and he had to leave. His anger had reached such a boiling point that the thought of staying in the UK was unbearable. I knew all this. But I spotted my chance to ask him some questions.

I couldn't hold back. I asked him, "So, upon arriving here, did you really need to go around Sarajevo trash-talking Mama and me, portraying us as the bad guys for not returning with you? You left us with your debt and refused to transfer the documents back to Mama's name, just to make things more difficult. You've been spreading your twisted version of events here, knowing full well it's not true. Why? To cast yourself as the victim when you're far from it."

He glared at me, his face turning red with fury, insisting I didn't understand anything. When I offered to show him the documents, he dismissed the offer with a sneer and said he wasn't interested. He started shouting, and I matched his volume.

After returning to the apartment, I told Husein I wanted to be driven to the airport to change my ticket and get an earlier flight back to London. I had no intention of staying. Husein managed to defuse the situation somewhat, but I couldn't wait to get back to London.

THE GREAT RECESSION

After wandering the historic streets of Sarajevo, I was about to embark on a new chapter: the unpaid internship at CNBC in London. The adventure kicked off with a whirlwind of excitement, which thankfully distracted me from the argument with my father. I had more thrilling things to focus on. The training was rigorous, but it was clear from day one that I was being set loose into the wilds of broadcasting with a significant amount of autonomy. My responsibilities were mine to command, without a safety net.

The newsroom was a bustling hub of activity, and the software we used, iNews, was a labyrinth of complexity. Back then, the digital age was just a glimmer on the horizon, and I was tasked with handling massive, cumbersome tapes. My mission was to shuttle these tapes to the editor, meticulously outline my edits, and then navigate the perilous journey of feeding the edited tape back into the system. I mastered this intricate dance so well that I soon became the go-to person for producers with high-stakes shows.

The real test came during the 2007–2008 financial crisis, a period of chaos and discovery. The air was thick with the tension of a world in upheaval. I seized the opportunity to engage with high-profile guests, delving deep into the crisis and developing a newfound obsession with crude oil, particularly Saudi oil. My days were consumed with absorbing every scrap of information from Saudi Arabia and OPEC. My passion shone through during a screen test with the bureau chief who told me I had the perfect face and voice for news. Sadly, there were no reporter positions available at the time.

In a surprising twist of fate, my Iranian British boss, recognising my dedication, crafted a one-year freelance contract for me, a rare opportunity amid the competitive landscape. But change was afoot. He soon left for another department, and I found myself under the scrutiny of a new English boss who had objected to having me as an intern back when I started. Despite my best efforts, every internal job opening seemed to go against me, often going to less experienced but privately educated candidates I had to train, yet who would leave after their six-month probationary period was up.

By November 2007, I had officially transitioned from intern to a salaried position. My new role came with significant responsibilities: pre-interviewing guests, feeding crucial information to presenters, and making editorial decisions. An English senior producer with a soft spot for me (due to her own Bosnian connections) became my mentor. She was a guiding light, teaching me the ropes of news writing and entrusting me with breaking news during live shows. Her mentorship was invaluable, and I thrived under her guidance.

As I delved deeper into the world of economics, I became fascinated by the forces that drove markets and the impact of oil prices on the US dollar. The low exchange rate made my long-awaited New York trip not just a dream, but a reality.

With the pound sterling strong against the dollar, I joked with my old university friend Leni, "Let's go and lift the American economy!" By this point she was engaged to her English boyfriend and wanted to shop for a wedding dress and bridesmaids' dresses. So, we packed light, planning to buy everything we needed in the Big Apple, although this trip was more than just shopping. It was an opportunity to explore as much as possible in five whirlwind days.

Leni and I were both fashion-conscious, so we made a list of places to visit and items to buy, in addition to shopping for her wedding dress. We rose early at six in the morning and set out for a delicious breakfast at one of the restaurants she had researched. After that, we enjoyed some sightseeing before diving into a day filled with shopping.

New York City was a dynamic blend of winter's chill and the city's ever-vibrant pulse. Despite the dry, sunlit winter, the city was alive with energy. We navigated the urban jungle by iconic yellow taxi, indulged in classic diner fare, and took in the Statue of Liberty. The highlight was ascending to the top of the Empire State Building, where the city's skyline was striking against the crisp winter sky.

Returning to London, I continued my journey at CNBC as the recession tightened its grip. The fallout from the economic downturn led to major shifts within the channel. Sponsorships were slashed, shows were cancelled, and staff cuts were inevitable.

But leaving all the troubles of the recession behind, I was back in Germany, this time for Leni's wedding. It was a whirlwind from the moment we boarded the plane. Somehow, the entire wedding party ended up on the same flight. It felt like a sitcom episode. Most of us even stayed at the same hotel, so it was like a never-ending reunion party.

We arrived in the evening, and the next day was all about church rehearsal. But in the morning seven of us squeezed into a car like Brussels 2.0, navigating busy streets while trying not to annoy the German police. At one moment, they were unhappy with us, so Leni had to play peacemaker, and somehow, we made it to the church. Inside, two priests—one Nigerian officiating in English and another in German—were ready to go. But did we rehearse? Not really! We were too busy catching up and laughing like we were in a Hollywood comedy.

At dinner time, we gathered for a pre-wedding feast. It felt fantastic to be surrounded by familiar faces, but soon enough, Leni and her fiancé needed some downtime, whereas the rest of us decided to hit the local nightclub. Little did we know that in this small town, the only club was filled with German pensioners who looked at us like we were aliens from another planet! Fifteen minutes later, we fled back to the hotel, where we stumbled upon Leni's future in-laws who had just arrived from Australia. Their stories were way more entertaining than our nightclub experience that felt like a mullet: business in front, party in the back!

The next day, after only three hours sleep, I headed to Leni's hotel room where all of us bridesmaids were to get ready. The atmosphere was electric with laughter as we hyped her up for her big day. The wedding itself was beautiful, but not only was I a bridesmaid, I also had an unexpected role as Leni's personal dress assistant. At one point, hours after the "I do's", I had to help her unhook her wedding dress so she could make a dash to the restroom. I'll never forget her jokingly saying, "God forbid anyone walks in while you're unbuttoning me!"

I was genuinely happy for her. She had found someone who made her smile more than I'd ever seen her smile before. And it was lovely catching up with her parents, who insisted I practice my German with them. I spent some time with other guests the next morning at a German spa and by the next morning headed back to London.

Not long after, Leni and her husband packed up and moved to Singapore. We kept in touch via Skype, which was a lifeline for our friendship.

⚜

By December 2008, the freelance gigs had dried up, and so had my time at CNBC. My job hunt resumed in a world where opportunities were scarce and businesses were shuttering. The relentless cycle of uncertainty seemed to stretch on forever. However, armed with my new experience, I thought I shouldn't have a problem finding a job.

During this period, an unexpected opportunity arose when Lauren, a producer at Fox Business Network in London, reached out to me. She informed me that my resume had caught their attention. It had been forwarded to them by an American war correspondent at Fox News I had initially connected with via Facebook, drawn by his experiences in Bosnia during the conflict.

My conversation with Lauren led to an exciting prospect: I was slated to join the network within a few months. However, the economic downturn threw a wrench in the plans, resulting in a hiring freeze. Despite this setback, I maintained contact with Lauren. Her warmth and kindness was a beacon in the often-cutthroat world of media. Her genuine nature left an indelible impression, making her seem like a rare gem in the industry.

I continued my search for a full-time job, in the meantime landing a temporary position at a shipping desk for oil reporting that my former CNBC colleague helped me get. The work was a monotonous grind; supply and demand were stagnant, and ships remained idle in port. A shipping trader I knew in Singapore shared that he could no longer even see the sea from his window, obscured as it was by the endless line of tankers. The prospect of economic recovery seemed like a distant dream.

Meanwhile, Frank's battle with his cancer had reached a heartbreaking point. Despite relentless surgeries, the scar tissue had grown too extensive, and the surgeons couldn't remove the rest of the cancer. Frank was initially admitted to Kings College Hospital, where Mama visited him daily, before and after work and on her days off. I was there often too. Later, he was transferred to the National Hospital for Neurology and Neurosurgery. After his final surgery there, he appeared to be on the mend. For a brief, hopeful week, we dared to believe he might be cured. He was vibrant, full of energy. But then, in an instant, everything unravelled. He fell into a coma, and the doctors delivered the devastating news to Mama that he would not recover. They advised disconnecting his life support. Mama, torn and grieving, consulted Frank's son and daughter-in-law (both general practitioners) who, with heavy hearts, agreed with the medical team's grim prognosis.

When Mama called me, her voice was shattered, and I could hear that she was crying. She asked me to come to the hospital because they were going to turn off Frank's breathing machine. His son reached out to his other siblings, and the doctors would wait for us all. I was numb, staring blankly at my computer screen, the unchanging market only deepening my despair. I told my boss, an American woman in her late fifties, who was visibly shocked and told me to take as much time as I needed, asking only to be kept updated.

As I gathered my things, she offered to call a taxi for me. I declined, needing the solitude of the train to clear my mind. Her condolences were the first acknowledgment of Frank's impending death.

Arriving at the hospital, I made my way to the private room where Frank lay. Mama and a nurse were already there. The hospital had arranged for a priest because Frank was a Catholic, despite his often-sceptical view of religion. Still, he deserved this final gesture of dignity.

The hours dragged by until his daughter and two sons arrived with their spouses. Frank remained connected to the breathing machine, Mama unwavering by his side. The doctors entered regularly, asking Mama to signal when she was ready for them to turn off the machine. Each of us took turns saying our final goodbyes, the room heavy with grief.

The priest's arrival marked the gravity of the moment. He offered words of comfort to Mama, explained the sacrament's significance, then turned to the rest of us before moving to Frank's side. The room fell into a profound silence, punctuated only by the rhythmic hum of the machine. As the doctors began the procedure, the priest led a prayer. I will never forget the haunting sound of Frank's last breath, the deep stillness that followed. We children, despite being heartbroken, stepped out to give Mama a moment alone with Frank. When she emerged, I held her tightly. She was crushed, her dreams of a peaceful retirement with Frank forever lost.

I helped Mama arrange the funeral, where I delivered a eulogy. The days that followed were filled with the unbearable weight of loss and the startling realisations that come with such profound grief.

My heart ached for my mother. The weight of Frank's passing hung heavy in the air, and I couldn't help but worry about how she would cope with the loss. Yet, beneath that worry, there was a flicker of admiration for her indomitable spirit. Mama was a force to be reckoned with, strong and resilient. Even in her sorrow, she understood the path ahead. She was acutely aware that she had to find her way through the shadows of widowhood, navigating the tumultuous waters of grief with a strength that inspired me.

PART V (2010–2017)

AND SO, IT BEGINS

Lauren, who just a year before had reached out to me for a job at FBN, emailed me to inform me of her departure from the channel for a new media opportunity, also in London, which meant we wouldn't work together. Despite this, we maintained our connection, often meeting for meals and catching up.

Lauren's background was a fascinating mix of Texan roots and British influence. Her distinct English accent was a result of her education in England, where she had lived as a child due to her father's career. The clarity and precision of her accent rivalled that of Jerry's from Northampton, creating an intriguing contrast with her Texan heritage.

Although our professional paths diverged, our friendship endured. Our regular lunches and dinners became a tradition, allowing us to stay connected and share our experiences. Lauren's blend of American and British qualities made our conversations both engaging and memorable.

FBN, where I was now to work, was based in Westminster, where snow was meticulously cleared for the delicate feet of politicians, unlike the rest of the city, which turned into a treacherous ice rink. Despite these challenges, I managed to make it to the building. There, I worked with an intern and an anchor who was also the Bureau Chief. Our three-person team curated news content tailored for a US audience, focusing on business affairs from the European Union.

My workday started at 8 a.m. and ended by 2 p.m., involving heavy liaison with the headquarters in New York who were a joy to work with. I enjoyed the job immensely, but it was short-lived. After the May 2010 UK General Election, Rupert Murdoch, the owner, decided to shut down the bureau, which meant more job hunting for me. I thought, God, not again! And so, my job hunt began anew, with few to no positive outcomes. In the eight years since I graduated, I had only three years professional experience and had completed thousands of job applications, not just in media but also for think tanks, charities, banks, etc. These applications went unanswered, or else claims were made that the application had never been received, even when I had proof to the contrary.

But by this time, it was time to head back to Sarajevo for my brother's wedding. Mama gave him £3,000 as a wedding gift to help cover the costs. Despite this generosity, we were treated like we didn't matter. There was a total lack of respect, especially toward Mama who had made a significant contribution despite Husein telling her it would be a small wedding, so she wasn't allowed to invite anyone. Yet, there was no such restriction placed on the bride's side, who invited whomever they wanted without contributing financially.

The day after the wedding, instead of meeting with Mama and me as planned, Husein and his wife went to visit her maid of honour, someone she could have seen at any other time. We were leaving Sarajevo the next day. It was becoming clear that she was helping distance Husein from us.

During this time Leni's husband messaged me to let me know she had gone into labour. I messaged back telling him to keep me up to date. Some hours later, she gave birth to a girl. A few days later, she asked me to be the baby's godmother, despite me being neither Christian nor baptized. I accepted.

Shortly after, Mama and I returned to London. With no end to my unemployment saga, Mama and I spoke about reaching out to our local member of parliament, as we believed he could help. We decided to make an appointment to see him. He was a prominent Conservative, once a Cabinet Minister. Our first appointment was at a local church, a common venue for MPs to hold their surgeries. We arrived at the cold, small church and took our seats. It was nothing special, no nuns or priests in sight.

While waiting, we noticed an older Englishman in a suit sitting opposite us. He had that deep British establishment aura about him and was watching us, not out of curiosity but with a kind of calculated intent. He tried to engage us in conversation with his posh accent, which was clearly out of place for that area. His questions were probing, subtly trying to extract information. It was obvious he knew who we were. Our phones had been bugged for years, so they knew where we were headed. We had learned not to share much over the phone, irritating them with our silence. This encounter was an attempt to intimidate us right before the meeting.

We were called in by the MP's researcher, a young woman of East Asian descent. She introduced herself and the MP, then began taking minutes, a common practice at these meetings. We told him about our case. He listened, seemingly unsurprised. We recounted how, just before Mama started working in the UK, her boss had received a letter from the Department for Work and Pensions advising him not to employ her. He ignored it and gave her the job, later telling her about the letter. The MP was particularly interested in seeing this letter. It was the only time he reacted, obsessed with the idea of it. He never dismissed its existence.

We then told him about all the strange occurrences that had been going on for years. Everything we discussed in our home seemed known to others, for example, people knew our bank balances, our comings and goings, that I was still unable to find a job. The bugging of our communications without legal justification, years after my father had left, implied either an unauthorised court order or illegal actions. Our phone would light up and beep late at night when it hadn't even been touched. We were often followed, and our personal details were manipulated and used against us. The MP listened, expressionless, while his assistant took notes. His look conveyed an unspoken acknowledgment, almost as if he was silently affirming our truthfulness. But he then made a bizarre comment. "Maybe the Bosnians are preventing you from working?" he said. I responded incredulously, "In Britain?" He insisted, "It is possible." I couldn't believe what I was hearing. "You're trying to tell me that the Bosnian government is preventing me from getting a job in the UK? The UK, a superpower, is allowing a small, powerless failed state to interfere in its system of government? Is that what you are saying?" He realised how absurd his remark was and fell silent. He had been desperately trying to divert the blame from the British establishment.

He then advised us to apply under the Data Protection Act to credit agencies, security agencies, and the police to check for bad credit or any records. Mama and I told him we had neither bad credit nor any records, not even a parking or speeding ticket. The meeting ended there, and we headed home to write to these institutions to prove him wrong.

Some months later, the official letters from all those agencies arrived, confirming we had no bad credit and no records. It was clear the MP had been trying to buy time. But why? What was he needing to investigate?

Life went on, and I continued to apply for jobs to no avail. My days blurred together, marked by persistent applications and a mounting sense of frustration. The disheartening reality of joblessness had begun to overshadow my life, and I felt trapped in a never-ending cycle of rejection and stagnation. It seemed that my best years were slipping away, spent in a futile pursuit of employment that stubbornly refused to materialise. My sense of isolation deepened, as no one seemed to grasp the full extent of my struggle; no one was walking in my shoes.

My heart ached with despair as I watched my friends living their best lives. They were working, savouring every moment and exploring the world, while I remained trapped in a cycle of financial struggle. The contrast between their freedom and my constraints was a constant, painful reminder of my situation. Even going to concerts had stopped. They were too pricey, and I had to watch every penny from my dwindling savings.

Mama's financial support, although a lifeline, felt like a dagger to my pride. The very thought of relying on her as an adult crushed my spirit and left me feeling utterly defeated. Each time I accepted her help, another piece of my self-esteem crumbled away, leaving me hollow.

My days became a relentless, soul-sucking routine of scouring every job site I could find. With each application I sent out, a tiny spark of hope would ignite, only to be extinguished by deafening silence or crushing rejection. The few responses I received seemed to mock me with their rehearsed excuses about hiring freezes, or that my application had not been successful.

It was as if the entire job market had conspired against me, united in their mission to keep me unemployed. The same lines repeated ad nauseam: "Hiring is on hold," "We'll keep your resume on file" and yet they would employ someone else. But the rejections echoed in my mind. The frustration built up inside me like a pressure cooker, threatening to explode at any moment.

This endless cycle of hope and disappointment was slowly eroding my spirit, leaving me angry, frustrated, and desperate for a break, any break, to escape this suffocating limbo.

My attempts to find work were relentless but ineffective. Each application seemed to dissolve into the void, leaving me at home day after day, enveloped in a dread that accompanied the monotony of my situation. It was a period of acute frustration and disillusionment, marked by the seemingly insurmountable challenge of finding meaningful employment.

Then, one day, when I was at my lowest ebb, a knock on my door offered an unexpected diversion. A Conservative Party candidate, campaigning for the London Assembly, stood there with an upbeat demeanour that contrasted sharply with the typical political persona. She had a bubbly personality, more reminiscent of someone not so Conservative. We struck up a conversation, and her questions revealed an uncanny understanding of my predicament. When she inquired about my current work status, I admitted that I was unemployed and struggling to find a job. Her response was both surprising and intriguing: "Why don't you come help me canvass the area? You can meet people, gain a different experience, and most importantly, get out of the house."

I was initially sceptical, and I remember telling Mama that this was not an innocent invitation. But the prospect of getting out of the house and engaging in something new was appealing. The opportunity offered a welcome diversion from the rut I was stuck in, so I decided to take her up on the offer but remain cautious. The timing felt unusual, as if this encounter was a sign that a different form of spying was on the horizon.

The weeks that followed were unexpectedly enjoyable. I found myself amidst a group of Conservative Party councillors and other campaigners from various areas who were all working to support the candidate. The experience was marked by camaraderie and laughter, with interactions far removed from the grim monotony of the job hunting I was still doing. At one point, Boris Johnson, who was campaigning for a second term as London Mayor, made a surprise appearance. The atmosphere transformed dramatically with his arrival, the area buzzing with energy as if the presence of a rock star had electrified the crowd. Boris, with his characteristic style—eccentric, animated, and somewhat disorganised—captured everyone's attention. I vividly recall a moment when a man halted his car in the middle of the street, ran over to Boris and requested a photograph with him. It was a spectacle that felt larger than life, a stark contrast to the dreariness of my recent experiences.

Boris's visit, although exciting, was brief, and canvassing continued in his absence. Our group later gathered at a local Indian restaurant, where an unexpected and unsettling incident occurred. Out of the blue, an Indian waiter revealed to me, in front of everyone and completely unprompted, that he had been part of Serbian General Mladic's army during the Bosnian War. The casual manner with which he made this revelation left me stunned. I couldn't comprehend how he knew about my Bosnian background because there was no visible indication of my heritage. In that unsettling moment, it became painfully clear that the invitation to canvass for this candidate was anything but innocent, just as I had suspected. It felt orchestrated, as if everything had been meticulously arranged.

I was troubled by the incident and decided to report it to a contact in the Home Office, but they indicated that without concrete evidence of him having been in the army, there was little they could do.

My attempt to address the matter with the Conservative Party's local chairman proved equally frustrating. The chairman, whose demeanour was dismissive and sarcastic, brushed off my concerns as a mere joke. When I pointed out that the waiter's knowledge of my background was troubling, he stumbled over his words before offering a token apology in the form of a free meal from the restaurant. My response was blunt: I refused their offer, feeling that their gesture was insufficient and dismissive of the serious nature of the incident. This encounter only reinforced my growing scepticism about the Conservative Party's commitment to addressing issues of racism and discrimination.

The situation added another layer of frustration. After a trip to Bosnia with Mama, we returned to find that various documents of ours had been tampered with. They were not as we had left them. We even found a bank statement next to the toilet. To make matters worse, some of Mama's clothes were missing. What was going on? I met with my MP again, who feigned concern and offered to help with my job search by requesting my CV. However, despite his assurances, no job offer came.

I had told him that I had been accepted into a master's program a few years back, but the offer had been withdrawn after the University of the Arts London (UAL) sent over some information about me. The university had refused to disclose the content of their communication. When I was a student at UAL, I had noticed false information on my file, such as the claim that I lived with Mama on income support, which was untrue. Mama was working and I was a student. No benefits were being received. Even the MP found this information peculiar and agreed that such data should not be part of a student file. He assured me that he would investigate the matter, given that British institutions were expected to adhere to certain regulations.

Despite his investigation confirming the inaccuracies in my student file, the university's handling of my subject access request was problematic. UAL initially claimed that the staff member responsible for subject access requests was on vacation, delaying the response period. When she returned, she allegedly hadn't opened my letter, causing further delays. The university then falsely claimed that my cheque for the request was insufficient, leading me to cancel the original cheque and send a new one. This appeared to be a deliberate attempt to stall the process.

I reported these issues to the MP's office, and he requested the name of the person to contact directly to expedite the resolution. UAL then asserted that the documents were stored elsewhere and would take time to retrieve. It became evident that the university was engaging in obstructionist practices to cover up their mismanagement and continue infringing on my rights. After six months of delays, UAL finally provided a minimal response consisting of just three pages of documents, far fewer than even an application for a university place would be.

In December of that year, I filed a complaint against UAL with the Information Commissioner's Office (ICO). The ICO ruled that UAL had not responded in a timely manner but took no further action. By this point, I had grown accustomed to the pervasive inadequacies and injustices in Britain, especially given the challenges Mama and I were facing.

During this period, a friend whom I had met while canvassing with the Conservatives encouraged me to run for MP, believing that my presence would bring valuable diversity to the party. Although I was initially hesitant, I eventually decided to give it a try, recognising that most candidates do not win on their first attempt. My friend helped me with the application process and introduced me to key people at Conservative Campaign Headquarters. However, I soon encountered subtle yet persistent discrimination. It felt to me that my Muslim identity was a barrier, and it seemed the party insiders felt more at ease with candidates who had similar backgrounds to them.

Despite my initial enthusiasm, the discrimination I faced disillusioned me. Although my experiences with the party had provided an opportunity to engage with new people and escape the monotony of job searching, it also highlighted a disturbing pattern of exclusion and bias. The connection I had found with the Conservatives was tenuous at best, and my engagement with them eventually became a point of contention.

Ultimately, my disillusionment with the Conservative Party solidified, and I chose not to pursue further involvement with them. My experiences had left me with a profound sense of disdain for their policies and attitudes. The party's failures and biases contributed to my growing conviction that they were a negative force in the country's political landscape.

THE GOLDEN OPPORTUNITY

It had been three months since we returned from Sarajevo, where I became an aunt and Mama became a grandmother. Husein and his wife had a daughter, and we spent some time with that adorable little bundle of joy. But we were back, as I was due to start my master's in Global Political Economy at City, University of London.

One evening around seven, it was pitch dark outside except for the glow of the streetlamps. By this time, Mama should've been home, and worry started gnawing at me. Something felt off. I called her several times, but she didn't answer. Panic hit me hard. Should I call her work? But no one would be there this late. I paced nervously around the house, messaging her over and over, but still, nothing.

Then, close to eight o'clock, her silver Toyota slowly pulled up in front of the house. I rushed outside and my heart dropped—the front of the car was badly smashed. I gasped, asking what happened, if she was alright. She looked shaken and simply said, "Let's go inside."

Once we were in the house, she explained that a driver had unexpectedly and illegally crossed the double yellow line in front of Mama, causing her to crash into him. The accident happened under a bridge with no cameras, and the driver had behaved threateningly. When Mama called the Metropolitan Police that evening for additional information, she was told that the other driver's car didn't even match the registration plates, that the plates belonged to a Fiat Fiesta and not the car she described.

We had an appointment with our MP shortly afterwards and we informed him about Mama's car accident. His reaction was chillingly indifferent. One would expect at least a modicum of concern, a basic human response, but he showed none. Even a stranger would ask if Mama was alright, but he just sat there, detached, and merely inquired if the police had been informed. His lack of curiosity about the incident felt as if he knew more than he let on. He treated us like we were wasting his time, yet he was the one doing nothing to help us.

He did offer one thing: a job at a think tank. So, I sent him my CV and waited. And waited. Nothing happened. One day, while he was out campaigning with his researcher, I greeted him. Despite my feelings, I maintained respect. Abruptly, he asked me, "Why aren't you responding to the emails that think tank sent you for a job? Don't you want to work?" His researcher interjected, "I told him, Nadina is always very prompt at responding and that you may not have received it." It was true; I hadn't. I explained that my emails were hacked, particularly those involving important communications like job offers. He remained silent. He didn't ask the police to investigate my email hacking, despite this being a golden opportunity to do so and one that was within his power. When I called the police myself, they were completely uninterested.

At one point the police told me to apply in Dubai. I told them I did, but my emails never reached their destination, hence why they should investigate.

Eventually, the think tank did contact me, but only for an unpaid internship, which I had to turn down as I couldn't afford to travel to central London without a salary. I had done my share of unpaid internships and needed a job. Fed up with the lack of progress, I decided to compile a list of lawyers specialising in human and civil rights. My first choice was Liberty Advocacy Group, known for defending ethnic minority human rights cases. When I called them, they advised me to request information under the Data Protection Act from my MP and hire a solicitor, but said they were at overcapacity and couldn't take my case. Every law firm I contacted claimed to be "at overcapacity", almost as if the response was orchestrated.

I formally requested all information from the MP's office under Section 7 of the Data Protection Act 1998, including notes from our meetings and a letter from Theresa May, the Home Office Minister at the time. She had written to the MP after he had requested some information about Mama and me. His researcher responded that handwritten notes were shredded once action points were completed. So, there was nothing. I consulted the library in Parliament by phone and Liberty Advocacy Group, and both found it surprising and suspicious that the MP refused to send me the documents. I needed those notes to take the matter to court, but he withheld them, intentionally preventing me from seeking justice.

A Somali British lawyer initially offered to help but then abruptly told me never to contact him again, likely after being pressured. Many law firms didn't respond to my emails.

This wasn't the only instance when my emails were clearly hacked. During the first term of my master's degree in London that September, everyone else received emails containing reading materials and other essential information for essays, except me. Upon investigation, the university discovered that only my emails were blocked from receiving study-related information. It became evident that, in addition to hindering my job prospects in the UK, someone was also interfering with my education.

Despite numerous letters sent to various Conservative ministers, and requests to hold a private meeting with the Prime Minister and Foreign Secretary, they refused, leaving us no option but to seek legal remedies, which were also blocked.

One day in December, we were awaiting an important call from Mama's probate lawyer, scheduled between 11 a.m. and 12:30 p.m. We were on high alert, ensuring that the phone line remained free and ready. We sat there anxiously, doing everything in our power to avoid any distractions and make sure that this crucial communication could come through. And yet the phone never rang.

Later, Mama received an email from the lawyer: "I have tried to call you several times, but your line has been constantly engaged from 11 a.m.–12.30 p.m." But the line had not been engaged. Not even close. We were not using the phone for any other calls. We were prepared for this call and had taken every possible measure to ensure it would come through.

It was infuriating beyond words. This wasn't a simple mistake or a minor lapse in communication. This was deliberate sabotage. There's no plausible explanation for why our phone was "constantly engaged" when we knew for a fact it wasn't. The fact that our communications were tampered with added a whole new layer of frustration. It felt as though they were playing a cruel, manipulative game, obstructing our access to vital information.

The more we dug into it, the more it felt as though we were entangled in a corrupt system designed to create as many obstacles as possible. It was outrageous and unacceptable. How many more hurdles would they throw in our way? How many more times would we be forced to confront this level of incompetence or deliberate obstruction? The knowledge that something so critical was deliberately obstructed was maddening. We were prepared, we were waiting, we did everything right. The interference with our communications was not just an inconvenience, it was a flagrant violation of our rights.

As midnight marked the end of a tumultuous year, I stood on the brink of a new chapter: my graduation from the master's program in Global Political Economy at the end of January 2014. Excitement surged through me as Mama joined for the ceremony; her joy made every late night worthwhile. The grandeur of Guildhall in London was the perfect backdrop as we introduced our families, sharing in our collective achievements. Clad in our gowns, we lined up, each handshake with professors a rite of passage. Yet, a shadow loomed. Although we celebrated, the weight of uncertainty hung over us.

A few months later, Mama received yet another frustrating email from her probate lawyer: "I have just tried to call you, but the number seems to be dead. Have you changed your number? Please call me."

We had not changed the number. The phone was not engaged at that time. Once again, our communications were being sabotaged. How many times did we have to deal with this blatant interference? The number was perfectly operational, but the lawyer's attempts to reach us resulted in a phantom dead line.

It's maddening to think about the level of depravity required to orchestrate this kind of persistent obstruction. What twisted games were they playing? Was this all some perverse amusement for them? Did they derive pleasure from making our lives more difficult and turning a straightforward probate process into a frustrating ordeal?

In Britain, the life of an immigrant is tragically undervalued compared to that of an English person, even when both hold citizenship. The disparity is stark and painful. If an English person faced similar hardships, the entire nation would rise in a tidal wave of support. But we immigrants? We're left to struggle alone in the shadows, our cries for help echoing in a void of indifference.

My heart ached with a desperation that seemed to know no bounds. The relentless interference in our communications was just the tip of the iceberg, a cruel reminder of the invisible forces working against us. Despite the triumph of graduation, the world seemed determined to slam every door in my face. Each job application felt like a plea, each networking attempt a desperate cry.

The agony of those fleeting moments of hope! Like a starving man catching the scent of a feast only to have it cruelly snatched away. LinkedIn connections sparked with promise, hiring managers showed interest, and for a breath, I dared to dream. But then, as if by some perverse cosmic joke, they would vanish into thin air or utter those soul-crushing words "your application was unsuccessful" or would never respond. Each time, it felt like a dagger twisting in my gut, a reminder of my powerlessness.

As another year drew to a close, desperation clawed at my insides. In a last-ditch effort to break free from this maddening cycle, I set my sights on a Temporary Communications Assistant position at the US Embassy in London, a lifeline I so desperately needed.

I clung to this application like a drowning man to a life raft, praying that it would be the key to ending this nightmarish witch hunt. The weight of my dreams, my ambitions, my very future hung in the balance. Please, I silently begged the universe, let this be the turning point. Let this be the moment when the tides of fortune finally shift in my favour, and I can break free from this suffocating limbo of rejection and silence.

THE JOB

In the first week of January 2015, I received an email inviting me to a work-related exercise at the US embassy at 10:45 a.m. sharp. The email was impressively detailed and organised with military precision, just the way I liked it. It specified that the assessment would last forty-five minutes and instructed me to bring two forms of ID: one for security and my passport. Additionally, the email mentioned a second interview a few days later, advising me to "tentatively keep some time available in your schedule to attend the interview day, in the event that you are contacted". Their specificity impressed me, and I complied with all the instructions.

On the day of the interview, I arrived at the entrance near South Audley Street with plenty of time to spare. As instructed, I reported directly to the security guard at the South Pavilion, avoiding the visa queue. The embassy security, all British, asked for my identification documents. They checked my passport and driving license, then handed me my passport back while keeping my mobile phone with my driving license in a small box. This procedure was new to me; I had never had to leave my phone at other embassies. But I complied without question, recognising that I had no other choice.

After passing through security, I went up the large, somewhat dirty stairs and entered the old embassy building at Grosvenor Square. I sat in the waiting area, the cold January day brightened by sunrays streaming through the glass. Soon, a woman from Human Resources appeared, her demeanour cold and unfriendly. She showed no interest in being professional or welcoming. Despite this, I remained professional and tried to converse with her.

She escorted me in a large lift to the assessment room, logged into a computer, and instructed me to follow the paper instructions and answer the questions. One question involved finding a quote by an ambassador on social media, a task a six-year-old could do. I completed the tasks ahead of time. She thanked me and said they would contact me if I passed the assessment. I thanked her and left the embassy, passing a marine stationed in a massive foyer before the reception area. I admired his unwavering stance as I exited the building, retrieved my mobile phone and driving license from security, and headed to Bond Street Underground station.

That same day, I was thrilled to receive an invitation for an interview. Despite the job being temporary, I saw it as a valuable addition to my resume. I prepared thoroughly for the interview a few days later and arrived at the embassy once again. After going through security and leaving my phone at the reception, I waited in the foyer for forty-five minutes past my scheduled interview time. No one informed me of the delay, despite the receptionist's calling HR twice to notify them of my presence.

Eventually, the same HR woman arrived and led me to an interview room. Inside, I found a group of people in their mid to late twenties with posh English accents. All were English, despite this being an American embassy. Trying to keep an open mind, I answered all their questions confidently. After the interview, HR took copies of my certificates and documents, including my passport and a form detailing my travels over the past ten years. The extensive documentation process made it seem as though I had already been offered the job. Why else would they need all those copies?

I left the embassy, retrieved my belongings from security, and noted the stark contrast between the sunny day of my first visit and the cloudy, icy cold day of my second. As I walked to Bond Street station, I turned on my iPhone, which was unusually hot and unresponsive. In the days that followed, my phone exhibited clear signs of interference. The device was constantly hot, even when idle. The battery drained quickly, the camera would activate at random, and data usage spiked without reflecting my actual activity. Turning it off took longer than usual, and I even noticed static noise in the background during phone calls. When I took it to the Apple store, the support lady's responses indicated that someone might have tampered with it. I realised that during my long wait at the embassy and then the copying of my documentation, someone might have had ample time to interfere with my phone. I'm sure the Americans at the embassy were unaware of this breach. What purpose would it have served them? After all, it was an official from the State Department who informed my father during the war that the British were tapping our phone.

Despite my confidence in my interview performance, I did not get the job. Further investigation revealed that the position went to another English person. It was clear that I never stood a chance.

Mama was upset and angry, while I felt exhausted by the ongoing abuse. When I informed my father, he contacted his American friends, all of whom had worked for the US government, who merely stated that employing local staff was normal. Being cc'd in the email, I questioned whether it was normal for almost all the embassy staff to be white English people, as if ethnic minorities didn't exist in the UK, and for those English staff to have political connections while making hiring decisions on behalf of the U.S. State Department. I knew this because I researched everyone working at the embassy. Surely if they preferred ex-Parliament staff, they should say so in their application, but then that would be discrimination. But isn't that also what they were doing, discriminating in favour of one group over another? Their lack of response confirmed my suspicions that nothing about those two appointments was genuine.

This experience highlighted the systemic obstacles I faced in the UK. My emails had been hacked before, and now my phone had been tampered with during a job interview. It seemed that every time I applied for a job where English individuals were involved, particularly those with connections to British MPs, I had no chance, regardless of my qualifications.

The interference with my communication continued to be a significant barrier, preventing me from securing employment. It was a clear violation of my rights, carried out under the guise of a "legitimate job interview". Despite my resilience, I couldn't help but wonder when, or if, this abuse would ever end. What on earth did they want? The war was over, my father wasn't writing anymore. Whatever connections he had been exchanging information with had nothing to do with me. The ordeal left me disillusioned and questioning the integrity of the systems.

Despite my relentless efforts, I was still trapped in a monotonous cycle of job applications. Each day was consumed by the tedious process of completing extensive forms, crafting cover letters, and tailoring my CV to fit the demands of each position. Yet, no matter how hard I tried, it became painfully clear that there were some powers at play that had no intention of letting me get a job in the UK. The futility of it all weighed heavily on me, leaving me disillusioned and questioning the very system I was trying to break into.

A few months later my brother, his wife, and their three-year-old daughter visited us in London. From the moment they arrived, tension filled the air like a thick, suffocating fog. I can still feel the shock that coursed through me when I caught my sister-in-law rummaging through my personal belongings. The invasion of privacy felt like a physical blow, leaving me feeling vulnerable and disrespected in my own home.

When I caught her in the act, I simply asked her not to go through my private belongings ever again, although the look of entitlement on her face made my blood boil. But it was my brother's automatic defence of her actions that truly shocked me. He behaved as if that was her birthright. How could he not see the blatant disrespect?

Mama was so excited at the prospect of spending time with her granddaughter, and it pains me to think of how that joy was tarnished by their behaviour. The image of my sister-in-law throwing a tantrum over the cost of tourist attractions is etched in my mind, a perfect encapsulation of her entitled attitude. The realisation that they expected us to bankroll their entire vacation left a bitter taste in my mouth.

They decided to sleep in the living room even though there was a bedroom available and made up for them. Each night they chose to go to bed at 9 p.m., but not to sleep. They would set up their inflatable bed in the living room so they could watch TV and not spend time with us. The thing is, Husein became a different person when he married. He had always blamed Mama and me because he didn't get a British passport, even though back in 1996, Mama had begged him to stay with us to complete his education and get the citizenship. He chose not to.

But it was the conversation about the surveillance that truly chilled Mama and me to the bone. My brother's casual acknowledgment of the fact that our home was bugged left us feeling betrayed and exposed. His nonchalant "I know they are bugging your home" echoes in my mind, a stark reminder of how far removed he was from our struggles.

Their abrupt departure, a week earlier than planned, brought a mixture of relief and sadness. As the door closed behind them, Mama and I felt a chapter of our life closing as well. The family we once knew and loved seemed to have disappeared, replaced by these inconsiderate strangers.

ECHOES OF BETRAYAL

As the beautiful sound of the ezan (adhan) drifted through the streets of Sarajevo, I woke up to a sun that seemed determined to chase away every shadow of the night. The ezan, a deeply ingrained part of Bosnian culture and religion, often felt like a celestial alarm clock, a reminder that a new day was beginning, one filled with its own promises and challenges. Mama and I were eager to seize the day before our planned meeting with my father. Our temporary apartment, perfectly located just a stone's throw from his place and around the corner from the US Embassy, seemed almost too convenient. We spent a few peaceful moments on the balcony, watching the city come to life, before we set out for our lunch meeting.

Our lunch was supposed to be a straightforward family affair, a rare opportunity for my parents to reconnect after years of estrangement. The thought of a relaxed meal, with my parents getting on, should have been a simple pleasure. But when we arrived at our chosen spot by the river, it became clear that this lunch would be anything but ordinary because sitting with my father was someone who would confirm more than I could imagine. The picturesque location, with the river's roar providing a natural barrier to eavesdropping, seemed to set the stage for a conversation that would unravel long-buried secrets and ignite deep-seated emotions.

As we settled in and ordered the lamb—an aromatic Bosnian delicacy that had been spit-roasted to perfection, its tenderness reminiscent of joyous childhood celebrations like Eid and May 1 celebrations at my uncle's country home—the atmosphere was initially serene. The lamb was succulent, falling off the bone with an ease that spoke of years of tradition and skill. It felt like a moment suspended in time, a calm interlude before the storm of revelations that was about to break. This wasn't the first time Mama and my father had shared a table since their divorce because they had also crossed paths at my brother's wedding in 2010. Back then, Mama was willing to put their differences aside for the occasion, but my father just couldn't help himself making comments to portray himself as a big man, a behaviour that Mama ignored.

Our conversation soon veered to my father's past work with *Ljiljan*. My father began recounting tales from his days at the newspaper. His voice took on a nostalgic tone as he described the daily operations of *Ljiljan*, the influential people he had met, and the lessons he had learned. Each story was laced with the intensity of a time when Bosnia was on the brink, and the stakes were unimaginably high. I listened, both fascinated and troubled, while he spoke of the pressures and the intricate web of politics that surrounded his work.

Then came a revelation that struck me like a bolt of lightning. "That's why the English bugged our phone in the UK, because they didn't like my writing," my father said casually. The table fell silent, the weight of his words sinking in.

He recounted an incident following the publication of his provocative article, "Power is the ultimate aphrodisiac—a glimpse into a political portrait: Who is the man who disregards small nations and peoples, using all his influence to advocate for the division of Bosnia and Herzegovina?" The article, published on January 8, 1997, had stirred up a hornet's nest. While my father was working in the *Ljiljan* newsroom in Sarajevo, a commotion erupted at the entrance. An angry man in a suit burst in, clutching a newspaper. The man's face was a mask of fury, his demeanour menacing as he zeroed in on my father.

He introduced himself as a high-ranking FCO official stationed in Sarajevo. With a commanding presence, he slammed the newspaper down on my father's desk and made his demand clear: "Stop writing articles about British foreign policy." My father's response was defiant: "Tell London to stop interfering in Bosnia, and maybe no one would need to write anything about your foreign policy." The official's rage was palpable. His face reddened, and he slammed the newspaper down again. His threat was chilling: "We know you have a daughter and an ex-wife in London. If you don't stop writing these articles, harm will come to them."

Upon hearing those words, the air seemed to tighten, becoming almost suffocating. A frigid wave of fear swept over me, leaving me stunned and paralysed. For a moment, time seemed to stand still. The world outside—the bustling city, the distant sound of the river, the everyday noise of life—faded into nothingness. The weight of the threat hung heavily in the air, each word reverberating with a chilling resonance. The gravity of the threat hit like a punch to the gut, leaving me gasping for breath, my heart racing so fast it felt as though it might explode.

Mama's face went ashen, her eyes widening in a mixture of horror and disbelief. Her usually composed demeanour shattered into a million pieces. She looked at my father with a combination of fear and anger, her lips moving soundlessly as if trying to grasp the full enormity of what had just been said. The reality of the threat was evident in her silent anguish, a stark contrast to the cold indifference my father displayed.

When I asked my father how he had reacted to the threat, his response was disturbingly nonchalant. "I didn't take it seriously," he said with a shrug. Mama's face mirrored my shock as she repeated his words. How could he be so blasé about something so grave? I felt a surge of anger that he had not treated the threat with the seriousness it deserved. He should have been furious at the official, not dismissive of Mama's genuine concern.

As my father continued his story, it became clear how deep the corruption and manipulation went. He explained how the FCO official had then visited President Alija Izetbegovic. The president, showing an alarming lack of backbone, had capitulated to the official's demands with disturbing ease. My father's old friends from his SDA days later confirmed that the meeting had been brief but decisive. The official had insisted on the removal of my father's column from *Ljiljan*, and the president had complied without protest. The betrayal was acute, and my father's time at the newspaper ended abruptly, a casualty of political manoeuvring.

My father's voice grew sombre as he revealed that, only weeks after leaving *Ljiljan*, American diplomats began probing into his sudden departure. It was an inquiry that eventually led to a shocking discovery. My father told me that a list containing names of foreign spies in Bosnia was accidentally published by American sources, and it included the high-ranking FCO official. It turned out he was an undercover MI6 officer. The realisation that an MI6 officer had threatened the safety of two immigrant women in the UK—Mama and me—was both terrifying and enraging. At the time the threat was issued, we had a permanent right to remain in the UK, which made the situation even more appalling. The British intelligence community had overstepped its bounds, threatened our safety, and exposed a severe violation of our rights.

Mama's distress was palpable. She said, "Of course, he would have the power to abuse our human rights in the UK and block Nadina from finding a job." The guest at the table, clearly aware of the broader context, added, "Not only did he threaten you, but he also made rounds threatening every journalist in Bosnia who dared to speak the truth about Britain and its interests. The unfortunate reality for you two is that you live in the UK, making it easier for the British establishment to overlook this coward's abuses."

The president's compliance with the FCO official's demands was disturbing, but the depths of the official's actions were even more shocking. The lengths to which the establishment went to undermine our rights and manipulate situations to their advantage were unfathomable. It was as though British spies were so thin-skinned that they could not handle even the slightest criticism of their foreign policy. If they wanted to avoid scrutiny, they should have remained neutral instead of wreaking havoc on innocent lives.

My father and I had a long-strained relationship, marred by his actions and decisions. This now added to it, like a final nail in the coffin. Even when we attempted to reconcile, his behaviour often reignited old wounds. His casual dismissal of the threats we faced, and the repercussions of his writings, felt like a betrayal. He never fully acknowledged the damage his writing had inflicted on our lives.

As I sat there, absorbing the gravity of my father's revelations, the full extent of the British government's actions against us became horrifyingly clear. We were not equal under British law, and the protection afforded to us was non-existent. The British establishment's actions seemed designed to keep us in a state of perpetual subjugation, denying us opportunities and freedoms that might have been available elsewhere. My repeated job applications to Dubai at the height of the migration, which went unanswered, suddenly made sense; my emails were never reaching their destinations, blocked by unseen forces.

It became evident that the British establishment had used its considerable power to oppress and control us, despite us having had no direct involvement in my father's writing. The letter Mama received around 2000, written by a child in Cyrillic alphabet, now made sense. Their bullying and harassment had already begun back then. Our lives had been turned into a nightmare by forces that saw us as mere pawns in a larger game. As September 2015 unfolded, it was clear that the struggle and the fight for justice were far from over. The shadows of our past were long, and the road ahead was fraught with uncertainty and unresolved conflicts.

MY FATHER'S ARTICLE

This is the original article in Bosnian, followed by my English translation. This article is what led to threats against Mama and me from a high-ranking FCO official based in Sarajevo.

Published in the Bosnian language on January 8, 1997

Power is the ultimate aphrodisiac—a glimpse into a political portrait:

Who is the man who disregards small nations and peoples, using all his influence to advocate for the division of Bosnia and Herzegovina?

A LEADING ADVOCATE OF BRITISH NEOCOLONIALISM
In Western politics, there is a permanent gene for the destruction, saturation, assimilation, if necessary, of the entire nation or nation in the name of its higher interests. This grotesque determination of the West in recent times was felt best by Bosnia, Rwanda and many other countries where the "civil war" erupted. In Bosnia, when military force failed to achieve the desired outcome, the West resorted to a policy of intrigue, its most insidious and dangerous weapon. Certainly, the main pillars of such a policy cannot bypass the British Foreign Office, or its branch Chatham House, headquarters of the Royal Institute for International Affairs, or the laboratory for the creation of "civil" and "ethnic wars." As one prominent historian put it, "At the heart of British politics is the act of doing harm to others." However, this does not reflect the views of the British people, who frequently voice their opposition to their conservative government. The Foreign Office, for years, has carried out covert actions, often through allies or agents abroad, far from the scrutiny of its own citizens.

CALL FOR THE DIVISION OF BOSNIA
British policy towards Bosnia during the aggression has been fully exposed, evolving from "naive ignorance of the situation

in the Balkans" to openly siding with the aggressor. When weapons and direct interference failed to achieve the desired outcome, a new strategy emerged: the policy of consensus. This British-invented tactic of covert operations aimed to undermine Bosnian authorities and institutions, culminating in an open call for mediators to partition the country in the name of "peace in the Balkans."

The most recent example of this undermining was the demand for the dismissal of Deputy Defence Minister Hasan Cengic, a key figure in the Bosniak resistance. To clarify, during the most intense fighting, Cengic reached out to John Shalikashvili, the US Chairman of the Joint Chiefs of Staff. He also sought assistance from the Iranians and anyone else who could help. The Iranians responded, providing weapons that helped protect the Bosniak people from further genocide. Now, the democratic West is linking this "Iranian connection" to the conflict, using it as a pretext to undermine President Izetbegovic.

The demand for Cengic's resignation can be traced back to the US Republican National Convention in San Diego on August 14, 1996. At that event, the stage was given to two individuals widely seen as bearing significant responsibility for the genocide in Bosnia: Lawrence Eagleburger and Henry Kissinger. Kissinger, who consistently called for Bosnia's partition (as we will later explore), and both men stressed that Bosnia would be "a matter of preference" for the next US president, putting heavy pressure on Clinton. In response, Clinton eventually, through Glyn Davies, a colleague of Nicholas Burns (who would later demand Hasan Cengic's resignation), confirmed that non-Bosniak soldiers had left

Bosnia, the "Iranian mujahedin" were no longer present, and weapons could now be unloaded at Ploce harbour. However, fearing the Bosniaks would align with American interests, British intelligence agency MI6 continued its efforts to associate Bosnia with Iranian mujahedin. The involvement of MI6 became evident as early as 1993, when they fabricated "Islamic fighters" to incite a Bosniak-Croat conflict.

On September 8, 1993, Henry Kissinger responded to Clinton's assertion about the disbanding of "Islamic fighters," advocating for a "realistic" American foreign policy toward Bosnia that accepted both its partition and the genocide. He argued, "The wisest and most historically consistent approach for America would be a referendum in each ethnic area, offering a simple choice between a multi-ethnic Bosnia and some form of division... A realistic, independent Muslim entity might be the most desirable outcome. This would be the best compromise between the principle of self-determination and long-term stability... There are no innocents in Bosnia."

BRITISH GENERAL

Who, exactly, is Henry Kissinger, and why is he so determined to partition Bosnia? Kissinger first gained prominence as National Security Adviser and later as Secretary of State under the Nixon administration. Born Heinz Alfred Kissinger in Germany in 1923, he was a German Jew who fled Nazi persecution and ended up working in a boar-bristle factory in Manhattan. After college, his proficiency in German earned him a spot in a special US Army training program, where he met Fritz Kraemer, head of a counterintelligence unit. Kraemer, a devoted Anglophile who studied at the London School of Economics, played a key role in introducing Kissinger to British intelligence circles even before the end of World War II. With Kraemer's recommendation, Kissinger enrolled at Harvard, where he was mentored by William Yandell Elliott, head of the government department and a staunch UK agent who had studied at Oxford. Elliott was a prominent figure in the Round Table movement, an organization founded in 1910 by Cecil Rhodes, a loyal servant of the British royal family. Rhodes' vision, as he stated, was: "I contemplated the existence of God, giving him a 50:50 chance of being real. What would God want for the world? He would want it to be well managed. In that spirit, I will work to further the British Empire and bring the entire world under British rule, including the recovery of the United States (the former colony), creating one unified Anglo-Saxon Empire."

THE GRAVE CONSEQUENCES FOR SMALL COUNTRIES AND SMALL NATIONS

It's worth noting that Kissinger became a member of the Round Table movement, later leading the American branch and promoting the British neocolonial system from 1952 to 1955. He also participated in group therapy at the Tavistock Institute in London, a psychiatric centre focused on psychological warfare and brainwashing. Influenced by these sessions, he adopted the doctrine of "credible irrationality".

The rise of British agent Henry Kissinger as a powerful influence in US foreign policy from 1969 to 1992 clearly illustrates the dominance of London and Washington since the assassination of John Fitzgerald Kennedy. From 1963 until Bill Clinton's election in 1992, no American president openly challenged London or the British crown on significant foreign policy matters. "While I was in the White House, I informed the British Foreign Office more effectively and directly than the US State Department," Kissinger stated on May 10, 1982, during a speech at the Royal Institute of Foreign Affairs (Chatham House) celebrating the 200th anniversary of the British Foreign Office. He admitted that nearly all major political decisions he helped shape in America were "British made". At this event, Queen Elizabeth II awarded him an honorary knighthood on the recommendation of British Foreign Secretary Douglas Hurd.

That same year, Kissinger established his private intelligence agency, essentially a miniature State Department, funded by several banks, including the Kissinger Association. Lord Carrington was part of the bank's founding board, and although he served for only three years, he greatly influenced Kissinger. Lawrence Eagleburger was the president of the Kissinger Association until he took on the role of National Security Advisor in the George H.W. Bush administration.

According to Douglas Hurd, the former British Secretary of State who praised him, Henry Kissinger, in his book *Diplomacy*, acknowledges a remarkable yet troubling synthesis of moral (sic!) order that is based on the dynamics of power rather than on the recognition of small nations and states.

"Power is the ultimate aphrodisiac," this influential figure once remarked. Given the number of countries he has destabilized, Kissinger is often seen as one of the more successful serial killers of this century.

This prospect of "Bosnia aligning with American foreign policy" is precisely what alarms London the most. Any effort to solidify a genuine alliance between Bosnia and President Clinton faced resistance from the "fifth column" of Kissinger, Gingrich, and Bush.

NEW ALLEGIANCES

Sitting across from my American friend W in our favourite coffee shop, with the rich aroma of freshly brewed espresso in the air, I felt a blend of gratitude and frustration. W's face was tight with anger as he vented about the unfairness of my situation, his voice cutting through the quiet murmur of conversations around us.

"Are they insane?" he exclaimed, his hand slamming down on the table, causing our cups to rattle. "What does your father's article have to do with you? This would never happen in the US!"

I felt a lump form in my throat, touched by his fierce loyalty and determination to help me. It was a stark contrast to the cold shoulder I was constantly receiving in my job search. As he outlined a potential job opportunity with a UK-based startup, I found myself torn between hope and scepticism.

The freelance producer role he described was far from my dream job in foreign policy, but beggars can't be choosers, right? I nodded along, forcing a smile as I agreed to take on the position. Inside, however, my heart sank at the thought of a detour on my career path.

As the weeks passed, I threw myself into the monotonous work, clinging to the lifeline it provided while never losing sight of my true passion. Our regular coffee meetups became a sanctuary, a place where I could momentarily escape the suffocating weight of my circumstances and engage in stimulating discussions about Obama's administration and the ever-evolving situation in Bosnia.

But with each passing day, a realisation began to take root in my mind, growing stronger until it was impossible to ignore: I no longer wanted to stay in the UK. The thought of leaving filled me with a mixture of excitement and guilt. How could I abandon Mama to face the abuse alone? And yet, how could I continue to live in a country that had so thoroughly rejected me? If I was to leave, Mama would have to come with me. It wasn't possible otherwise.

The UK, once a place of promise and opportunity, now felt like a prison. My dreams of making a name for myself here had withered and died, replaced by a burning desire to seek greener pastures elsewhere. As I reflected on my CNN internship in 2002, the clarity I'd gained then only solidified my current resolve. The US beckoned, a beacon of hope in the darkness that had engulfed my career.

Fuelled by a potent cocktail of anger and determination, Mama and I embarked on our own investigation into the high-ranking FCO official who had threatened us. As we peeled back the layers of his past, a sense of vindication washed over me. His retirement, his return to train civil servants for embassy positions, coinciding with the timing of my own application process with Civil Service. I suspected my name must have stood out to him, making it nearly impossible for me to succeed in that process. He later ran for a seat in government but was unsuccessful. It all painted a picture of a man whose actions had not only impacted my career prospects but had ultimately led to his own downfall.

Our detective work didn't stop there. We dug deeper, uncovering a web of betrayal that left me reeling. Friends and family members we had once trusted had sold us out, aligning themselves with those who wished us harm for their own gain. The sting of their treachery was sharp, but it only strengthened my resolve to forge ahead. Those so-called friends had provided photos of us, where we went out and who was with us. They used all this to completely isolate us.

In the face of the continued abuse, I channelled my energy into a new obsession: Russian foreign policy. I had spent time talking to my father's American friend who had worked in US foreign policy and who advised me to take Russian foreign policy more seriously as it would be a big topic. So, I did, and with it the Russian language too, which came easily to me, a small mercy in a world that seemed determined to throw obstacles in my path. I threw myself into studying Russian President Vladimir Putin's speeches and interviews, finding a strange comfort in the familiarity of the Slavic tongue.

As I delved deeper into the intricacies of Russian geopolitics, I couldn't help but daydream about the possibility of interviewing Putin himself. The thought sent a thrill through me, a reminder of why I had fallen in love with foreign policy in the first place. The world was vast and complex, full of fascinating stories waiting to be told. How could I possibly content myself with the narrow confines of UK-centric work?

Amidst all the turmoil, life marched on. It had been seven years since Frank's death, and Mama and I had moved into a new home, where things took a disturbing turn. We began to notice small but telling signs of illegal break-ins, such as missing items, even food disappearing. One day, bizarrely, the kitchen faucet shot up water when turned on. It had been working perfectly until the day before, and we were told there were signs of it having been tampered with. Then, overnight, our kitchen flooded because the water pipe connected to the washing machine had been tampered with too. Someone clearly had a key to our home, though we hadn't given one to anyone. Was it from when we changed the locks? Or had it been copied from the locker? We had no idea!

I threw myself into my studies and work, and Mama busied herself with endless home improvement projects and working. Her resilience never ceased to amaze me, even as I watched her meticulously tend Frank's grave, a task his own children ignored.

My relationship with my father, once a source of pride and inspiration, had deteriorated to the point where I could barely stand to hear his name. The revelation from the previous September had driven a wedge between us that seemed insurmountable. I asked Mama not to mention him to me, unable as I was to reconcile the chaos his actions had wrought in our lives.

As I juggled my production job, Russian studies, and dating, a bright spot appeared on the horizon. An unexpected reunion with Ben, the son of my French teacher Mary from Trinity School, brought a welcome dose of nostalgia and possibility to my life.

Over dinner with him and his American wife, we caught up on the years that had passed, and I found myself opening up about my secret passion for photography. The idea of exhibiting my Bosnian photos, capturing moments of beauty and struggle in a land that had shaped me so profoundly, filled me with a nervous excitement.

As I listened to Ben talk about his life—his teaching career, his love of sailing, stories about his sister Ruth and his parents, Mary and Tim—I felt a genuine happiness for my old friend. His life seemed so straightforward, so uncomplicated by the weight of international politics and family legacy.

Yet as we parted ways that evening, I felt a sense of optimism. My path may have been more challenging, more fraught with obstacles and betrayals, but it was uniquely mine. The world of foreign policy, with all its complexities and dangers, still called to me. And though the UK had turned its back on me, I was determined to find my place in the global arena.

As I made my way home that night, the streets of London felt different somehow, like a temporary stop on a much longer journey. The future, with all its uncertainties, beckoned. And for the first time in a long while, I felt ready to answer its call.

PART VI (2017–2018)

A JOURNEY INTERRUPTED

My earliest memory of my father dates to when I was around four or five years old. Sometimes Mama would take me to a crèche, and sometimes that responsibility fell to my father. One late autumn morning is particularly etched in my memory. I wore my red wool coat, and my hair was neatly tucked under a soft woolly hat. We walked hand in hand down a tree-lined road covered in changing leaves. He was on his way to work. The road was flanked by Austro-Hungarian–style buildings, houses, and white fences from the empire's era. My father would always have green minty bonbons in his trouser pocket and would share half with me. Their green wrapping and minty taste are fond memories. We would walk hand in hand, talking. I was a chatterbox who early on learned to use technical terminology as if I were a philosopher of languages.

On days when he finished teaching early, he would pick me up from the crèche or from my grandmother's and we would head to a nearby restaurant while Mama was still at work. The owner knew my father well and always saved him the same table. Like clockwork, whenever we arrived, the table was available, seemingly kept just for us. My father, always in his suit, and I, in a pretty dress chosen by Mama for crèche or days at Grandmother's, would sit and enjoy our time together. My father would order mezze, including smoked Bosnian meat, cheeses, and ajvar, a Bosnian red pepper relish. I would always order crêpes with chocolate and shaved walnuts, sometimes with a scoop of ice cream, depending on the season.

These cherished moments became distant memories when the war started. I think I lost my father to the war when we were refugees. We became like acquaintances. In the UK, our lives diverged further, his consumed by the Bosnian War and mine by school and news, because I aspired to be a journalist. When he left for Sarajevo, it was as if we were strangers.

One cold January afternoon in 2017, I received a text message while preparing to see my university friends at a reunion in London, our usual venture on the first Saturday of the year. The message stopped me in my tracks. I turned off the music, stared at the phone, and then slowly made my way downstairs. I opened the white wooden-framed glass door to the living room, feeling somewhat in shock, my stomach in knots. The room felt warm, and the TV was on. I lowered the volume, and with Mama's inquisitive gaze on me, I said calmly and woodenly, "Hasan died."

Mama responded, "Which Hasan?"

"My father," I replied.

Her shock was palpable, more intense than mine. She seemed speechless for a moment. When she finally spoke, she asked, "Who told you?" I showed her the text message from Husein. He hadn't called, just texted, as if casually informing me of an acquaintance's passing. The method of this news delivery felt like a declaration of my unimportance.

Mama told me to call Husein, and I did. His phone rang without answer. I then called my father's phone, only to discover it was now with my sister-in-law's father. Reluctantly, he put my brother on the line. Husein's demeanour had changed after his 2010 marriage, and their 2015 visit to London had added to his atrocious behaviour toward us. His coldness reflected the influence of his wife, who tried to sever my and Mama's relationship with him. Husein sounded uninterested, answering my questions impatiently, eager to hang up. It was a moment when he could have shown character and humility, but he chose rudeness and abruptness, as if blaming me for our father's death.

My father died from heart failure during a freezing week in January. I later learned that extreme winter conditions can often lead to death in older people with heart problems. Several others had passed away from the same cause that week. He had high blood pressure, ate fatty foods despite his doctor's advice, smoked compulsively, and enjoyed whisky, all habits that led to his demise. He died on his living room sofa, watching his favourite documentary about African wildlife. Earlier that day, he had coffee with his best friend, a night editor of Bosnia's daily newspaper. His life, spanning seventy-two years, ended one winter afternoon on a sofa in Sarajevo.

When I called Tanja to inform her, she told me Husein had called her two hours before texting me. By this point Tanja had become increasingly distant from me, influenced by my father who she idealised. She gossiped about me every chance she had. Knowing two hours before me that he had passed away, she didn't think to tell Husein to reach out to me. But on the line with Mama and me, she explained how Husein found our father.

Husein received a call from his father-in-law, who heard a phone ringing inside my father's apartment but got no answer at the door. Husein rushed over, used his key to gain access, and found our father unresponsive. After checking for a pulse and finding none, they called the police and ambulance. He was pronounced dead and taken to the morgue.

It was a Saturday evening. I cancelled my plans with friends. My French university friend called to offer condolences—a gracious act. We spoke briefly, and he told me to call if Mama and I needed anything. He was more compassionate than my brother. My other university friend, a Danish Italian, called too and kept checking in on me. In the days to come, others called and messaged as well, especially family friends and those who knew us from the war era.

Mama and I sat in silence, shocked. Then a call came from Husein, asking if I would attend the funeral. I said yes but needed a few days to find a ticket. He said he spoke with Tanja, who had the same response, and set the funeral for Tuesday. Muslims are usually buried the same or next day, but this was a different situation.

Finding a ticket was challenging due to heavy snow in Europe, but I managed to book a flight for Monday morning via Germany, returning on Thursday. The weather worsened, and I kept receiving updates throughout the night that my flight departure time kept getting pushed back. Early morning on the way to the airport, the snow was so heavy that the taxi driver nearly skidded off the road while driving me to Heathrow. Upon arriving at the airport, it felt like I was the only one there; flights were continually cancelled or postponed, and people were leaving to wait elsewhere. It felt like one of those abandoned airports you see in horror movies. I approached the check-in counter and asked the agent about my flights. She explained that my flight time had already been changed three times due to extreme conditions in mainland Europe and snow on the tarmac at Heathrow. When I asked if the flight would depart at all, she said they were monitoring the conditions and couldn't give a definite answer but advised me to check in regardless. That gave me hope. I checked in and went through security. Holding my cup of coffee, I, along with others, stared at the flight information board. Most flights continued to be delayed or cancelled.

After hours of waiting, I finally saw the dreaded notification: My flight was cancelled. The news hit me like a punch to the gut. I approached the airline counter telling the lady I needed to get to Sarajevo for my father's funeral the next day. Her eyes softened with sympathy, and she promised to check for alternative flights. But with the severe weather gripping the UK and mainland Europe, there were no flights leaving London that day.

I begged her to look for options for the following day. She found a few, but the earliest one wouldn't get me to Sarajevo until well after the funeral, in the late evening. She warned me that even those flights were far from certain, given the heavy snow affecting Germany and Bosnia as well. The weight of the situation sank in, and I felt the crushing reality of how little control I had over getting there in time.

I was upset, but I knew it wasn't her fault or the airline's. Flights from Britain are sometimes cancelled at the slightest snowfall, but this was more than just a dusting—the airplanes were covered in snow.

I waited hours for my luggage before heading home. The next day's flights were also delayed or cancelled. I couldn't attend my father's funeral. Mama was upset that I couldn't go; she also wanted to attend, but at such short notice could not get time off work, and realistically, we both knew the weather was beyond our control.

People kept saying I needed closure, but I was left wondering what that even meant. Death is the final chapter, whether or not you have closure. My relationship with my father had been fraught, marked by endless arguments over how his writing had impacted my career. He never once acknowledged the fallout of his words, always placing the blame squarely on me, especially for not returning to Bosnia with him. He never seemed to care about how his decisions affected Mama and me in the UK. To him, I was just someone who should take some inconsequential job and not bother with education, while his son thrived in Bosnia, courtesy of our father's connections.

Months later, I had to sit through the reading of his will in Sarajevo, despite being entirely excluded. The probate lawyer made a point of rubbing it in that I inherited nothing. Tanja later told me that my father had secretly left a significant sum of money to my brother, despite claiming he had no money and despite the probate lawyer telling me there was no money, just an apartment. It was the same old corrupt game that seemed to define Bosnia. I confronted my brother, and he panicked, stumbling over excuses and asking who told me. The money and the apartment were his now. In 1996, Mama had given her share of the Brcko apartment to him, which allowed them to buy a new one in Sarajevo. Legally, I was entitled to a share, but my father had given his portion to my brother. But it wasn't about that—it was the complete absence of any acknowledgment or message for me. What stung was the lack of any final words that might have shown some remorse for the pain his actions had caused me. The actions whose consequences I bore.

SREBRENICA

The sound of silence was eerie. Not even the gentle breeze was audible. My footsteps made no sound as I walked along the path between the graves. People were present, but their words were indistinct, as if muffled. The grass had grown tall, and trees were in full bloom, aging like the memorial itself, which stands as a sombre tribute to the victims of the Srebrenica genocide. After visiting my father's grave in Sarajevo, this was the first time in three days that I found some semblance of peace. Here, among the murdered civilians who were killed solely for being Muslims, the noise finally subsided.

As I moved among the graves, I touched the smooth tops of the Nisani, the white upright tombstones inscribed with the names of the deceased. From one side of the memorial, a sea of white tombstones stretched out. Another section carried the engraved names of victims, some belonging to families where over twenty members were killed. Entire generations were wiped out in a few days. I wondered how the Mothers of Srebrenica felt when they visited this place, seeing the graves or the names of their loved ones on the monument. The entrance to the Srebrenica Genocide Memorial was a sombre and reflective space dedicated to honouring the victims whose remains have been recovered. However, many mass graves, including those from Srebrenica, remain undiscovered throughout Bosnia.

When I turned around, I saw a sea of graves under the setting sun. In any other place, the early warm evening might have been a beautiful sight, but here, it was the Potocari Srebrenica Genocide Memorial. Even the beauty of the setting sun couldn't diminish what I was witnessing and how this visit would impact me.

I wandered through the memorial, feeling as if I were the only person there. A man signalled me to come over, and for a moment, I stood rooted to the spot. He approached and asked if I wanted to join a talk with one of the mothers. I thanked him and followed him to the front of the memorial.

I joined others sitting in front of an older woman, close to her seventies but looking older. She wore a skirt and a shirt, with a scarf covering her hair. She began to recount the events of July, 1995, the last time she saw her two sons and husband. She described them as if they were standing right in front of her. Perhaps their spirits were there, though we couldn't see them. She spoke of her children the way only a mother can, calling them by their first names and recounting how she hugged them and refused to let go until Serb forces forcibly separated them. Her husband had told her not to worry and to seek safety. She hugged him, and then they left forever, never to be seen again. For her, the memory of her family remains vivid. Though their remains age, their spirits stay forever young in her mind, as she last saw them. Each time she tells her story, she seems to age another decade, the lines on her face bearing witness to her suffering.

Like so many other victims, her sons and husband were killed in July 1995, a massacre that the International Criminal Tribunal for the Former Yugoslavia ruled as genocide in 2004, a ruling upheld by the International Court of Justice in 2007, which found Serbia guilty of inaction.[18] Under the command of General Mladic, Serbs from Serbia and Bosnian Serbs separated men and boys from their female relatives. What followed was unimaginable, mirroring the atrocities Jews faced during World War II. In just a few days, over 8,000 Bosnian Muslim men and boys were slaughtered by Serbian death squads in Srebrenica. To conceal their crimes, the bodies were buried, exhumed using excavators, and reburied in secondary mass graves, making it difficult for families to find their loved ones' complete remains. Some graves at Potocari Memorial contain partial remains because families were told they might never find the complete bodies. Some were told they might never find any remains at all, and others are still waiting. Remains were identified by DNA and recognised by the clothes the victims wore the day they were murdered. Some of these remains are stored in the Podrinje Identification Centre in Tuzla, a site I visited the following day. There, I saw parts of a skeleton lying on an examination table—legs, an arm, a shoulder, and hips—belonging to a victim of the Srebrenica genocide. The rest of the body was elsewhere, in another mass grave yet to be discovered.

The old woman didn't have the complete bodies of her sons either. One was missing a skull, the other arms. It felt as if part of their souls were here at the memorial, while the rest lay in some cold grave waiting to be found. Bosnia sometimes felt like one massive grave, soaked in the blood that hadn't dried from all the victims of the Bosnian War, not just Srebrenica.

Listening to the woman's story, I was reminded of the days I sat in my living room in London, flipping through news channels to learn what was happening in Bosnia. It took me a long time to visit the Potocari Memorial Centre and to fully confront the weight of the Bosnian War. How could such cruelty exist? Do such monsters still walk among us? The answer is always yes. Many perpetrators have yet to answer for their crimes. Concluding her talk, the old woman said, "I died the day they were killed. My body is among you, but my soul is buried with them."

I thanked her for her time and headed across the street to a building exhibiting photographs of the day genocide became part of Bosnia's history. A choking sensation overwhelmed me as I entered. The weight of the history pressed down on me. I climbed the stairs and moved from room to room, reading descriptions of the photos on the walls, which told the story of the people of Srebrenica and their tragic fate. Silence reigned as I progressed through the rooms. Eventually, I reached a hall with seats in front of a monitor.

I sat down, and a documentary began. As I watched, the tightness around my chest grew, making it difficult to breathe. When the documentary ended, I felt dizzy in the warm room and struggled to see the exit. I walked faster, finding the stairs I had come up by. Someone asked if I was okay, and I gasped, "I need air." I rushed down the stairs and finally emerged into an open area, almost like a field. The silence was still oppressive. I took a few deep breaths, and slowly, the tightness and dizziness subsided when I was handed a cup of cold water.

I decided to walk around the memorial area, where Srebrenica families once sought refuge among the Dutch battalion, who failed to save them in 1995. Now, in 2017, the place was silent and empty, as if the tortured souls of the Srebrenica victims were the only inhabitants. The memorial site felt like a town where no one lived, where innocence perished, and where the world's media only remembered it once a year, if at all.

That day in May 2017 changed everything for me. Visiting the memorial, one cannot remain the same. As a child of the war, I had seen various aspects of the conflict through people who visited our home, but Srebrenica revealed the worst of humanity. The videos of the Serbian paramilitary unit known as Scorpions, which finally resurfaced through the efforts of brave Serbian human rights activist Natasa Kandic, showed the summary execution of Bosnian Muslim men and boys, killed for being Muslims. Serbia's goal was to ethnically cleanse Bosnian Muslims to create their long-held dream of Greater Serbia. During a speech in the Serbian parliament in 1995, Aleksandar Vucic stated, "For every Serb killed, we will kill one hundred Muslims."[19] At the time, he was a prominent figure in the Serbian Radical Party, which was allied with Slobodan Milosevic's regime. Vucic served as the party's general secretary and is known for his nationalist rhetoric during the Bosnian War. Today, he is the President of Serbia and his nationalistic rhetoric and lies against Bosnia continue.

Srebrenica profoundly impacted me, fuelling my passion for defending Bosnia's war victims and the country itself. For this, I have faced vicious verbal attacks, but I simply ignore them. What matters most is keeping the memory of the Bosnian War alive and hoping someone out there learns a lesson to prevent its repetition. Sadly, no one ever seems to learn from the gruesome events of history.

Srebrenica exposed the depths of evil that exist among us and the atrocities people can commit. We tend to believe such horrors can only happen in distant lands, yet similar events have occurred throughout history: to Armenians, the Holocaust, in Rwanda, against Yazidis, in Cambodia, East Timor, Uganda, Burundi, Rohingya, and most recently in Gaza, and Lebanon is headed in the same direction. Watching Gaza on television is like watching Bosnia all over again. The phrase "Never Again" doesn't seem to apply universally.

REFLECTION

I returned from Srebrenica with a weight that seemed to press on my very soul. The images of the mass graves, the unspeakable atrocities committed by the Serbs, haunted me relentlessly. Srebrenica was not merely a place on a map, it had become a symbol of the deepest, most harrowing cruelty humanity could inflict. It was a grim echo of the darkest chapters in European history, a genocide that stood as the most tragic event since the Holocaust.

In the days after my return, Tanja reached out to me on Skype, her voice a tentative thread of connection to the world outside my sorrow. She wanted to hear about my trip, to understand what I had witnessed. As I began to speak, I found myself lost in the recounting, my words spilling out uncontrollably, driven by an urgent need to unburden myself. I spoke for what felt like hours, describing every harrowing detail and raw emotion. Mama sat beside me, her presence a silent testament to her support, yet her silence only deepened the sense of tragedy. Tanja listened with a heavy, contemplative silence, absorbing my words without a single interruption. It was as if I was reliving my trauma through this one-sided conversation, and they seemed to grasp my need for this cathartic release, this desperate sharing of my soul with those who cared.

As the days dragged on, my mind remained ensnared by painful memories of Srebrenica. Then came a call from an Englishman working with a genocide remembrance organisation. He asked if I would speak to Türkiye's English channel, TRT World, about a recent Dutch court ruling. The court had ruled that the Dutch were only responsible for a small fraction of the lives lost during the Srebrenica genocide, thereby absolving them of responsibility for the countless others who perished. I agreed to the interview, though it felt like a bitter reminder of a similar experience from when I was fifteen, speaking to Channel 4 News about the Bosnian peace accord. Once again, I was cast in the role of representing my country, an honourable assignment and this time as a newly minted analyst, but more than anything, as a Bosnian who was exhausted by the Netherlands' weak excuses and their fragmented sense of accountability.

In the sombre confines of a small studio, I sat beside Shiulie Ghosh. Her eloquence and knowledge were matched by my own deep sadness, a reflection of the grief that had consumed me. I was tired, tired of the ongoing struggle for justice, tired of the Dutch trying to distance themselves from the tragedy they had a hand in. Ghosh began the interview by questioning whether the court's ruling, which had taken an eternity to reach, was adequate and what my thoughts were on it. I had long believed that no ruling could ever be enough. The Dutch needed to acknowledge their full responsibility, and so did the international community, which had been aware of the impending attack and did nothing to stop it. This was textbook genocide: the systematic extermination of a group based on their ethnicity or religion.

As the interview drew to a close, my thoughts drifted back to the time I sat across from Zeinab Badawi in 1995. At fifteen, I had faced her with the same gravity that now marked my expression with Shiulie Ghosh. Leaving that studio, I had felt a fleeting sense of pride, a belief that I had spoken for the victims, that my voice might have made a difference. My parents' friends in the US had praised my analysis, and I had felt a momentary surge of pride, believing I had defended the helpless. Now, however, the hollow feeling of futility seemed to pervade my efforts. Diplomatic answers, I was convinced, led nowhere. I was determined to be direct, unflinching, and unafraid of disapproval. I wanted to keep the memory of Srebrenica alive in the media, even if it meant facing hostility.

Upon returning home, I poured my grief into an article about the upcoming anniversary of the genocide. I needed a platform to share it, and as if by some twist of fate, a message appeared in my LinkedIn inbox from a Turkish woman connected with Türkiye's Anadolu Agency. She had seen my interview and praised my performance. We exchanged contact details, and as the anniversary approached, I asked if AA would consider publishing my article. The following day, she informed me that my piece would be published and that I would receive a contract to become their freelance London Correspondent. I felt a glimmer of hope, a fleeting sense of relief that perhaps the darkness was lifting. My article, "Remember Me When I'm Gone," was published on July 12, 2017. I was told it stirred deep emotions in many at the AA newsroom. In the months that followed, it opened new doors for me, allowing me to continue writing and commenting on Bosnia. Despite this small victory, the weight of my sorrow and the enduring quest for justice lingered, a constant reminder of the profound loss and the ongoing struggle for recognition and accountability.

HELL IS EMPTY AND ALL THE DEVILS ARE HERE

Mama and I were in Sarajevo for a family reunion with Husein and Tanja. It had all been going well, until the morning of the fourth day, when Tanja abruptly left without a single word of goodbye. We were stunned. Despite my frantic attempts to call her, the line was dead. My WhatsApp messages were met with only a solitary tick. That afternoon, while Mama and I sat in our hotel room, I called Husein in a desperate bid to understand what had happened. To our utter shock, he told us that Tanja had flown home to Berlin. We immediately asked why. What could possibly have prompted such an abrupt departure? Our thoughts turned to my Aunt Rahima, who had suffered two strokes and was under the care of a nurse while Tanja was away. Was this sudden move somehow connected to her condition?

Husein's response was as disconcerting as it was unexpected: "Your comments on her daughter's manners." I was taken aback, unable to comprehend how he could possibly know about a private conversation. Mama quickly interjected, "She didn't mention anything about that to Tanja. We only talked about it to each other when we were alone in our hotel room two nights ago." Husein's reply, "I know," was delivered with an unsettling calmness that sent shivers down my spine.

How could he know? He wasn't present when I made those comments. My mind spun with questions, each one more perplexing than the last, and I found myself grappling with the unsettling realisation that answers might remain elusive. Why would Husein have this knowledge? Mama and I had harboured suspicions about him since 2015, when he and his family visited us in London. Mama had confided in him about our fears, saying, "They are bugging our communications." His chillingly nonchalant response had been that he knew about it.

The situation grew even more suspicious when our planned lunch with Husein and Tanja's family on Bjelasnica Mountain was abruptly cancelled. This was just two days after my comments in the hotel room. Despite my repeated attempts to get an explanation, I received no answers. Tanja had been fully aware of the troubling activities directed against Mama and me. She wasn't innocent in this. Tanja was fully aware of every detail of our case. Her close relationship with my brother meant she was part of the discussions about what I had said. It seemed they had a private conversation, where they probably talked about how my comments had come to their attention. Their inability to be discreet was almost laughable, but the situation was far from funny. The level of their incompetence was almost comical in its absurdity.

When the call ended, Mama said, "This hotel room is bugged. How else would they know what you said? They couldn't wait to isolate us." I sat on the edge of my bed, struggling to piece together the fragments of this unsettling puzzle. My comment had been about Tanja's daughter's behaviour, which I had only discussed with Mama in our hotel room. The previous evening, she had acted out in a way that seemed more appropriate for a toddler than a fourteen-year-old. She had whined about not receiving any presents and incessantly demanded that I buy her things. She would frequently pull on my arm or show me what she wanted me to purchase, interrupting my conversations with others. To her mother, this behaviour might have seemed normal, but I had said nothing inflammatory in the hotel room, only that if she went through life with such an attitude, she wouldn't get far. Realising that a version of events had somehow been conveyed to Tanja was like a sudden, jarring revelation that finally made the pieces fit together.

We decided to meet Husein for coffee. Normally, we wouldn't have ventured out for coffee in the sweltering Bosnian summer heat, but Mama and I were desperate for answers. We arrived first and sat under a gazebo at a café outside the shopping centre. When Husein arrived, he seemed distant and unwilling to engage, as though he wished he were anywhere but there.

We began the conversation about Tanja's abrupt departure, and I pointed out that the only way she could have known what I said about her daughter was if our hotel room had been bugged. This theory was reinforced by the mysterious malfunctioning of our room's water system after we had gone out to eat, which forced us to switch rooms. I also mentioned that Tanja had blocked me on all social media platforms and her phone. Husein's response was chillingly casual: "Yes, your room is bugged. The British are bugging you here too. What do you expect?"

What do I expect? The realisation that our private conversations were being monitored felt like a gut-wrenching betrayal. Had Mama and I done something to deserve this invasive scrutiny? Mama's voice was sharp with anger as she demanded, "So if you knew, why didn't you tell us?" Husein's nonchalant reply was, "What do you think?"

I was stunned by Husein's casual acknowledgment of the surveillance. Mama and I had been aware of being bugged in the UK, but we never imagined it would extend to Bosnia or that my brother would be so openly aware of it. His indifference to the invasion of our privacy was deeply unsettling. It seemed that with our father gone, he felt more liberated to go along with these intrusions into our lives. The notion that the British felt entitled to bug rooms in foreign territories was shocking. It suggested an assumption that Bosnia was somehow an extension of British jurisdiction, allowing foreign authority to extend its influence into another country.

The most profound impact was the betrayal I felt from my brother. On that day in August 2017, I felt as if I had lost him. For Mama, it was the loss of a son. As for Tanja, her actions had rendered her a mere footnote in the larger narrative of betrayal and deceit that had unfolded. The pain and disillusionment were overwhelming, and the quest for answers seemed as elusive as ever.

Growing up, my brother and I shared a bond that was both deeply affectionate and playfully antagonistic. We were inseparable, always teasing each other, but it was the kind of teasing that only deepened our connection. I eagerly anticipated our adventures in Bosnia as adults: partying with his friends, who had become mine as well; driving through picturesque landscapes; and exchanging jokes and stories about our lives. I would rap badly along with the latest hits on the radio, and he'd give me amused side-eyes. In return, I offered advice about his romantic interests, while he tried to set me up with his friends.

One hilarious memory that stands out happened when we stepped out of Sarajevo International Airport on a scorching 40°C day. I was in a dress, desperately trying not to dissolve into a puddle of sweat. As I locked eyes with an Italian guy, I didn't realise he was part of a line of Italians waiting to head home after some sort of training. When he flashed me a smile, his buddies immediately jumped in with the usual flirty lines, treating me like some sort of international treasure. I kept walking but couldn't resist turning back to enjoy the spectacle. I gave them an amused smile.

My brother, witnessing this spectacle, was torn between cringing and cracking up. With a look of sheer panic mixed with amusement, he leaned over and said, "If anyone asks, we're definitely not related." It was a classic sibling moment, embarrassing but completely hilarious. Every time I think about it, I can't help but laugh at how my brother tried to disown me in public while all I was doing was keeping up with our two countries' diplomatic charm offensive.

These memories are precious to me, filled with joy and laughter that reflect the special bond we shared. But now, looking back through a veil of disbelief, I'm haunted by how drastically things have changed. Shakespeare's words from *The Tempest* resonate perfectly: Real evil doesn't lurk in some distant Hell, but among us, in those we once trusted.

DISCOVERING LOSS

A couple of weeks after our reunion, a sudden impulse led me to Google my Aunt Rahima. I didn't expect to uncover much, but something inside me had nudged me to search her name. I typed her full name into the search bar and hit enter. To my shock, her name was linked to an article in *Avaz*, a Bosnian daily newspaper. Aunt Rahima had never given any interviews, so seeing her name there felt unusual. My heart sank as I clicked the link, and there it was: her photo, accompanied by a death notice stating that she had passed away in Berlin on August 26, 2017. I discovered this on September 1.

Mama was sitting across from me in the living room, the same spot where I had delivered the news of my father's death just eight months earlier. My stomach churned and my voice trembled as I broke the news to her. "Aunt Rahima has died," I said softly. Mama gasped, her face contorting with shock. I turned the laptop around so she could see the screen, and she asked me to read the death notice aloud.

With each word I read, my voice cracked, unable to hide my own grief. By the time I finished, Mama was visibly distressed, sitting hunched in the centre of the sofa. Her eyes brimmed with tears, and her voice broke into a sob. I sat beside her, with one hand on her shoulder and the other clutching the laptop as I showed her the notice again. We both struggled to accept that Aunt Rahima was gone, despite knowing she had been ill and bedridden for years. The last time Mama and I saw her was over Skype just before our family reunion in Sarajevo. She had barely recognised us but looked lost, lying in bed while Tanja held the phone up to her face. We had hoped to visit her before the year ended. We thought a visit might bring some comfort.

Our mourning was tinged with disappointment and frustration toward my brother. He had failed to inform us of Aunt Rahima's death, a courtesy I would have expected, especially given his habit of sending messages for such news. Instead, I had to learn of her passing through a Google search. It felt like a cruel twist, uncovering such significant news in an impersonal way.

Mama and I sat together, reminiscing about the times we had shared with Aunt Rahima. We recalled her vibrant presence and the many memories we had: vacations by the sea, Brcko, and the laughter they had shared. I recounted my last meeting with her in Berlin, remembering her frailty and how we had envisioned a meaningful visit that never materialised. We held our own small memorial for her, reflecting on her life and her suffering. Though her passing left a void, we found solace in the thought that she was finally at peace.

Aunt Rahima had likely been buried in Berlin, though Mama and I didn't know the exact location of her grave. This left us unable to pay our respects in person. I recalled how, months before Aunt Rahima's death, Tanja had taken my late father's cat to see her. Tanja had told me that Aunt Rahima had understood and cried upon seeing the cat, recognising that her brother was no longer with us. Perhaps this realisation contributed to her passing.

Aunt Rahima and my father had shared a close bond, though it was marked by frequent arguments. I remembered Husein recounting a time when Aunt Rahima visited Sarajevo, and she and my father had bickered about something trivial. Their communication was through Husein, who had to relay messages back and forth between them, creating a comical yet poignant scene that I wished I had witnessed.

I messaged Husein to confront him about his failure to inform us, expressing my frustration at having learned of Aunt Rahima's death through Google. I told him that his behaviour was appalling and lacked basic decency. Unsurprisingly, he never responded. Perhaps he and Tanja thought that Mama and I would never find out.

Despite the disappointment and sorrow, Mama and I found comfort in reminiscing about Aunt Rahima's life. We shared stories of her strength, resilience, and the joy she brought into our lives. Aunt Rahima had always found ways to bring laughter and warmth, even in the darkest times. Her kindness and humour were qualities we would always cherish, and her memory would live on in our hearts.

In the end, we found solace in the knowledge that her suffering had come to an end. Her journey had been fraught with difficulties, but she had faced them with dignity and courage. Finally, she could rest, free from the pain that had marked her later years.

Cases like hers exemplified the struggle Bosnian women faced in a society where discussing wartime sexual abuse was taboo. The perpetrators of such crimes were often glorified, even by Western media outlets. This stark contrast between the silencing of victims and the lionising of offenders underscored the urgent need for us to advocate for justice and recognition, challenging the pervasive culture of silence surrounding these atrocities.

Despite the harrowing events of the summer, I knew I had to move forward with my life. I couldn't dwell on the past; I had to focus on shaping a future for myself. On November 23, 2017, I returned to TRT World to discuss the guilty verdict of General Mladic, a convicted war criminal. This was just days after I interviewed Serge Brammertz, the Chief Prosecutor of the ICTY, as the tribunal was winding down its operations. Contrary to the harsher portrayals I had heard, I found Brammertz to be remarkably kind. He performed his role with dignity, despite the constraints imposed by the international community. During his time, ICTY was the first international criminal tribunal to enter convictions for rape as a form of torture and for sexual enslavement as a war crime, a crime against humanity and genocide.[20] It recognised rape as a weapon of war and a tool of ethnic cleansing, rather than just an individual crime.[21] Brammertz's candour and generosity with his time were refreshing. Some years later, standing before the global media, Brammertz would assert, "The Bosnian War was not an internal civil war but an international conflict where the political elites of neighbouring countries played a significant role."[22] This was a sentiment we Bosnians had long understood, though the international community was reluctant to acknowledge it.

Around this time, the BBC invited me to discuss the Bosnian War and General Mladic's conviction. I agreed, and the interview was scheduled for the following week. However, the BBC, true to form, began airing a special report on General Mladic during their flagship News at Ten program. The segment, which featured interviews with Serb war criminals who had been involved in the atrocities, was deeply troubling. I was baffled as to why the BBC editorial team would prioritise their views. To me, this was not objective journalism but a clear attempt to present a distorted narrative. Throughout the Bosnian conflict, the BBC had consistently failed to report impartially. They portrayed General Mladic as a victim rather than a perpetrator. For a week, their primetime coverage seemed intent on presenting an alternative, misleading view of General Mladic as a figure to be admired rather than condemned.

When the BBC announced they would re-broadcast the same biased segment on the day of Mladic's ruling, I decided to withdraw from the scheduled interview. I emailed the BBC producer to explain my decision, noting that the broadcast was minimising General Mladic's crimes and promoting him as an innocent figure. I pointed out that although the interview with Mladic was scheduled for peak viewing hours, my interview was to air early in the morning when fewer people would be watching. This, I argued, was not objective journalism but a deliberate attempt to sway public opinion.

The next morning the producer called me, asking why I had pulled out. I reiterated my concerns, emphasising that the BBC's biased coverage was harmful, particularly given their history of Islamophobic reporting, which could foster further animosity against Muslims.[23] That evening, the segment was indeed pulled from the broadcast, which I took as a small victory. An American university friend congratulated me, stating, "It's either the war criminals or the victims or survivors telling the story. The media cares about ratings. Keep raising your voice, or they will get off easy. You forced the BBC's hand. Great job!" His support was encouraging, though I remained perplexed by the BBC's approach and could not understand why some Bosnians still chose to appear on such programs. To me, it seemed like a futile effort for fleeting visibility compared to the more significant, damaging coverage of General Mladic being presented as a hero.

I continued to write and analyse issues related to Bosnia, striving to fill the gaps left by mainstream media. I regularly pitched article ideas to Anadolu Agency, feeling that Turkish media had not adequately covered Bosnia. On one occasion, I was asked to write about Russia's investments in the energy sector of Republika Srpska, an entity created out of genocide in Bosnia. I crafted the article objectively, relying on factual information and insights from experts. However, the liaison from AA informed me that they could not publish the piece due to their diplomatic relationship with Russia. This was the same article they had specifically requested. When I expressed my dissatisfaction, the liaison's response was brusque, suggesting that if I was unhappy, I could resign. I was taken aback by such unprofessionalism. It became apparent that my rising profile as a writer and commentator had ruffled feathers within the British establishment. Despite this, I did not resign, but my communications with AA ceased. They used the very article they had requested to silence me, revealing their unwillingness to confront sensitive issues honestly.

Just before the year drew to a close, I found myself compelled to reach out to a former Bosnian diplomat. I felt an urgent need to share the harrowing experiences Mama and I had endured at the hands of a high-ranking official from the FCO. With careful precision, I detailed every unsettling incident that had transpired. His response was swift and chilling: He confirmed that the FCO official in question was indeed capable of everything I had described. In that moment, another piece of a complex puzzle fell into place, validated by those who had also faced this official's troubling conduct.

PART VII (2018–2024)

RESILIENCE IN THE FACE OF ADVERSITY

During a conversation with an American human rights lawyer who had faced the British government in courts on many occasions, I was hit with a revelation that left me stunned and heartbroken: I was on a no-hire blacklist in the UK, a direct consequence of the articles my father wrote criticising British foreign policy. The man behind this list was the high-ranking official from the FCO who had once threatened my family and me back in 1997.

The moment I heard this, I was overwhelmed with a deep, shattering despair. Tears streamed down my face as I grappled with a torrent of emotions: anger at my father for drawing such ire, fury toward the British establishment for its vindictive actions, and a profound sense of hopelessness about my future. The realisation that my hope of working in the UK in my chosen field had been irrevocably shattered was crushing. As I reflect on this revelation, I felt a wave of shock and disbelief washing over me. My mind reels, struggling to process this information. A no-hire blacklist? For me? The very thought sends a chill down my spine. How could this be? I didn't write that article. I had nothing to do with it. Yet here I am, punished for something entirely beyond my control.

As I reflected on the 18,000 job applications I had sent, each one in vain, my sense of despair only deepened. It felt as though every effort had been futile, every hope dashed by a system that had long since decided my fate. The weight of this injustice was almost too much to bear, leaving me grappling with a profound sense of helplessness and disillusionment.

A whisper of hope reached me from an American friend seasoned in the US Army's labyrinthine contracting world. The External Research Associates Program (ERAP) at the Strategic Studies Institute of the US Army War College (US-AWC) beckoned, a chance to step through doors that had remained shut in the UK.

Mama and I were absolutely over the moon at this opportunity! Even though it would be based in London, the excitement bubbling inside me was undeniable. Here was a glimmer of promise from across the Atlantic, a chance to seize what had eluded me elsewhere. It felt like the winds were finally shifting in my favour, and I could sense that this was a pivotal moment in my journey. I could feel energy coursing through me, igniting a spark of determination. This was more than just a job; it felt like a chance to reclaim my path and embrace the future I had envisioned.

With every passing moment, my enthusiasm grew. I could see the possibilities unfolding before me, and I knew I had to seize this chance with both hands. Mama's eyes sparkled with joy as we discussed the potential it held, and her unwavering support fuelled my confidence even more.

This was it! A chance to step into a new chapter, to pursue my dreams, and to make meaningful strides in my career. The thought of it made my heart race with excitement. I felt ready to take on the world, and I couldn't wait to dive into this opportunity that felt so right.

For some time, I had watched the ERAP from afar, waiting for its gaze to fall back firmly upon Russia. With meticulous care, I crafted my proposal and submitted it as July's warmth gave way to August. By September, I received word from the USAWC that my proposal had been accepted, and a research grant was bestowed upon me.

The news brought both elation and humility. Among the six chosen grant recipients that year, most were military personnel. I conversed with a high-ranking US Army official, ensuring that my research aligned with their interests while preserving the essence of my original proposal. This flexibility granted me the freedom to delve into the evidence with an open mind, though the core idea of my work remained steadfast.

I embarked on an extraordinary research journey that was so thrilling, I often woke in the middle of the night with new ideas for interviews or insights to explore. Every moment of this adventure was a sheer delight. I meticulously compiled a list of potential interviewees, each more significant than the last. The pinnacle of this quest was securing an interview with Alexander Nekrassov, a former Kremlin advisor. His contact, provided by an academic colleague in London who had connections within his circle, was a crucial key to unlocking the complexities of Russia's intricate web.

In January 2019, as day softly transitioned into night, Nekrassov asked me to call back after 7 p.m., assuring me he would grant me as much time as I needed. His perspectives on Russia were both profoundly valuable and thrillingly familiar to me. I had long admired his audacious interviews on British TV, where his distinctive Russian accent boldly challenged British politicians with uncomfortable yet necessary truths.

Our conversation was nothing short of mesmerising. Despite some of his answers being so lengthy that I hesitated to interject, the flow was smooth. Nekrassov wasn't just a keen analyst, he had insights far beyond what any article could offer. He unveiled the Kremlin's narrative with a vividness that portrayed Russia as a wounded bird floundering amid geopolitical storms. His candid discussion about Russia's diplomatic manoeuvres, especially its attempts to influence political dynamics in the Balkans, was riveting. He expressed concern about the potential destabilising effects of EU and NATO expansion, contradicting the typical Western narrative. This perspective perfectly aligned with the current situation in Bosnia, where Russia's interference was disrupting regional politics.

Despite his controversial politics, I found his insights on Russian foreign policy to be invaluable. His talk further fuelled my deep fascination with Russia that soon surpassed my interest in the Western Balkans. I was captivated by Russia's intricate history and its complex approach to international relations, aspects that the West often struggled to comprehend.

I also had the honour of interviewing Mo Sacirbey, the former Bosnian wartime Ambassador to the UN, whose work during and after the Bosnian War commanded my deepest respect. His reflections on the Dayton Peace Agreement and Bosnia's current state provided vital context for my research.

My investigation wove together threads from Russian media, former Yugoslavian news sources, Western media,

US Congressional hearings, and the occasional article from Mama. I would often jest that she made an excellent researcher, one I didn't need to compensate.

I valued the professionalism and support offered by the US Army while I navigated this new terrain. By May 2019, I had completed my research, culminating in a document titled "Bosnia, Russia, and the Terrorist Equation: The Implications for European Security and U.S. Interests." The work expanded to illustrate Russian interference across the former Yugoslav republics, revealing Russia's broad influence. This study was crafted for the US Army and policymakers, aiming to shed light on the complex interplay of geopolitics and security.

A few months later, I began to see articles in Bosnian press referring to changes brought on by the US Embassy. The changes were the exact recommendations and points I had made in my research for the Army and US policy makers. It was as though the US embassy to Bosnia had embraced my insights and elevated their most crucial elements. I knew I did a good job, but the fact that the issues I addressed were being used without anyone notifying me felt a bit like someone else was taking the credit. A former consultant, linked with an American intelligence agency and familiar with my research, remarked on the revelations within my monograph, telling me he checked out everything I wrote and confirmed their accuracy. He displayed a sense of surprise that I had such information.

In a later conversation with the American friend, I sensed his exhilaration over my completed 15,000-word research and recommendations. He optimistically believed that this prestigious addition to my resume would unlock doors for employment in the UK. Yet, despite this illustrious achievement, the doors remained stubbornly shut.

Seeking respite after such intense work, Mama and I ventured to the Bahamas, a long-held dream finally realised. As I swam far from the shore into the deeper depths of water, a magnificent manta ray glided toward me. Bahamian children on a nearby boat called out, urging me to move slowly to avoid a close encounter. I was startled for a moment. But the manta ray, with its graceful, majestic form, and non-threatening behaviour evoked a serene beauty that I had always admired. Its resemblance to the Northrop B-2 Spirit, an American heavy strategic bomber, in its sweeping, wing-like design, was striking.

During my USAWC Russia research I also looked at military equipment and fighter jets, so this encounter felt laden with symbolism. I turned to face the manta ray, marvelling at its gentle nature. Just as the B-2 Spirit commands awe, so did this manta ray, embodying an elegance that felt almost otherworldly. As I swam away, the manta ray followed, a silent guardian ensuring my safety until I neared the shore.

Some three months later, the COVID-19 crisis unfolded worldwide. British Prime Minister Boris Johnson introduced a series of lockdowns, albeit later than some experts had advised. These restrictive measures were designed to curb the spread of the virus, prohibiting people from mixing with those outside their households. A stay-at-home order was imposed, allowing people to leave their homes only for essential reasons such as buying food, medicine, or exercise, while Johnson partied in Downing Street.

During this period of confinement, I suddenly had an abundance of free time, despite my ongoing work on Russian foreign policy projects. With Mama's workplace closed and her on furlough, we were now constantly at home. The lockdowns felt reminiscent of house arrest. As we entered the second week, the UK experienced an unseasonable heatwave, giving it a summer-like atmosphere.

We took advantage of this time by undertaking home improvement projects, painting both the front and back façades of our house. We also engaged in extensive housework and gardening, including a thorough spring-cleaning of our wardrobes.

I maintained my fitness routine, albeit with modifications. I skipped rope in the garden, lifted weights, and did various other exercises. Mama and I alternated cooking duties. I perfected my butter chicken recipe, whereas she prepared traditional Bosnian dishes. We kept up with the news and basked in the sun on the numerous pleasant days. My work on foreign policy remained a constant, uninterrupted aspect of my life, a pursuit I found immensely satisfying.

But that June, I formally requested a change of surname. Since 2016, I had been working under my new surname after the tax office informed me that as long as I paid taxes, the name I used professionally didn't matter. Many people in the media worked under different names, so I decided to shorten my surname. I wanted to make this change official as I no longer wished to be associated with my father. His actions had caused me significant hardship and pain and ruined my chances of finding permanent employment in the UK. I simply didn't want to be called by his surname anymore. Within two weeks, I received the certificate confirming my surname change, allowing me to update documents such as my driving license, passport, tax records, banking details, and more. Completing this process felt like a great weight had been lifted from my shoulders. It was something I needed to do for myself to move on.

A few years earlier, when I gave an interview to TRT World using this new surname Ronc, Tanja and my brother criticised me. They seemed to think I needed their permission to decide what I wanted to do with my life, including what I called myself. I ignored them; after all, it was none of their business.

During the eighteen months of lockdowns, Mama and I were confined to our house like everyone else. I constantly followed the news and the death rates. I wondered how people in Bosnia, especially the elderly, were faring. The Bosnian economy wasn't strong and relied heavily on tourism, which had come to a halt. Fortunately, the US government, the UAE, and Saudi Arabia came to the rescue with a good supply of vaccines and other medical supplies.

Many friends reached out to Mama and me to make sure we were alright. Even some acquaintances sent emails checking in on us—beautiful gestures from those I hardly knew. I also reconnected with S.W. after we had lost touch. But my brother never called. I thought this was a prime opportunity for him to reach out, to fix the situation, but he never did. By this point, he had moved to the Netherlands and had blocked me on social media. But Mama and I didn't expect anything else from him. He showed who he was, and there was no going back from that. The bond between us had shattered, leaving us as strangers. In his eyes, we no longer existed, and we reciprocated that sentiment. Our estrangement was so complete that I now feel like an only child, with just Mama by my side in this fractured family portrait.

NAVIGATING HOSTILITY

Since my father passed away, I'd carved out a niche for myself as a political analyst specialising in Russian foreign policy. But landing a job in the UK remained a constant challenge. I'd also been searching for opportunities abroad, but since COVID, the job market felt sluggish or non-existent. The transition from President Donald Trump to the President Joe Biden administration brought changes that significantly impacted funding for research projects, leading to a decline in the external work opportunities that had become my saving grace. Although I worked on another large project, there was no pay until it was finished. I resolved to take any job that could supplement my income while I continued my new Russia research.

I reached out to Omer, an old university friend who was now serving as the Deputy Director General of TRT, Türkiye's national broadcaster. After sharing a brief version of my job search struggles with Omer via a message, he called me a week later. We chatted like old friends, and he told me to send him my CV, which I did the same day.

I didn't envision myself at TRT World long-term. The thought of working in television again as a producer was soul-destroying. If I was to stay there, it would have been for only a year or two to give me time to also finish my book before moving on to something more aligned with my passion for writing and analysis.

During this time, I was also healing an injury, which happened as I was headed out of the house for a run. Stupidly going down the stairs in my socks, I slipped and fell. It took a few stairs before my fall broke. The consequence, which wasn't obvious until the next day, was a severely bruised tailbone that left me in unbearable discomfort. The agony was constant. I could only sleep on my right side, propped up by six pillows for support. Sitting was only possible on a special cushion and a hard chair.

Two weeks after the fall, my doctor urged me to start moving. "Go for a walk," he said, but even that was exhausting. On one of my painfully slow walks in the early days of my injury, I vividly remember being overtaken on the pavement by a very old pensioner. The women shot me a bewildered look, like, "Seriously?" I spent more time roasting myself over how slow I was than I did complaining about the discomfort. Even the doctor had to bite back a laugh. The physio? Oh, she didn't even bother—she straight-up laughed.

Slowly, I tried. A month in, I found some relief through daily YouTube exercises, simple routines that did more to ease my pain than any painkiller ever could. The need for a faster recovery was due to an upcoming job interview after I was contacted for a job at a consultancy seeking an analyst on Russia's foreign policy and Europe. It felt like a glimmer of hope. The interview was via Zoom, with the head of HR, a fabulous lady who instantly made me feel at ease. At one point, she joked about the apple juice sitting on her desk, visible on camera, assuring me it wasn't whiskey. I laughed and quipped back that my water wasn't vodka either. It broke the ice, and we fell into an easy, lively conversation about life, work, and my aspirations. A few days later, I got the news: She had absolutely loved me and thought I'd be a perfect fit.

As is standard for such positions, there was a test given by the head of a department. The HR part was over. I was asked to complete a written test—a prediction of Europe's situation over the next six months. I dived in, consulting think tanks and various sources as recommended. I poured everything I had into that analysis, but in the end, they told me I didn't get the job. My predictions, they said, were too alarming. Ironically, as the months went by, my predictions proved to be correct. This whole experience revealed the disconnect between my insights and their expectations, perhaps influenced by their close ties to the UK Foreign Office, who was one of their clients. But I was past being surprised by these outcomes.

Meanwhile, my injury lingered. Eight weeks in, I began physiotherapy. It would take a full fourteen weeks before I truly felt better. Now, I descend the stairs slowly, slippers on my feet, always careful, each step a reminder of how easily life can change in an instant.

Three months later, I met with TRT World's London bureau chief, a Turk with prior experience working in London. He had received an email from Omer recommending me for a job. During our meeting, we discussed my experience and the political landscape of Türkiye and Bosnia. He then introduced me to the executive producer (EP), an Englishman who initially appeared friendly. Despite my extensive experience, he expressed he'd train me to update my knowledge on iNews, a newsroom software I hadn't used in almost eleven years, and other tools used at TRT World. He assured me of the necessary training once I started, though no start date was provided immediately due to his impending vacation.

Finally, in September, I began as a freelance Output Producer. To my surprise, I was assigned a beginner's role akin to that of a news assistant, a position I had held as an intern at CNBC fifteen years earlier. My responsibilities were even less significant than those during my internship at CNN. The initial warm reception had turned frosty, and it quickly became evident that the EP didn't want me there. He seemed intent on making my role so dull that I would leave voluntarily.

For four weeks, the EP refused to train me, leaving me idle in the newsroom. Despite my repeated requests to write or contribute in some capacity, he consistently declined. The only time I felt somewhat engaged was when working with a program editor awaiting his visa to Istanbul, who tried to reassure me about the training.

Eventually, an American program editor awaiting her visa took the initiative to train me, defying the EP's reluctance. The bureau chief then told me that I needed to master iNews to be promoted to Deputy Program Editor. Despite starting with four days a week, I reduced it to three temporarily to complete a US-based project, with plans to return to four days the following month.

After just two days of working on iNews, the EP summoned me to a meeting room and informed me that he wasn't impressed with my performance and that I should not return. I challenged his assessment, pointing out the lack of training and the unrealistic expectations: "You refused to train me for four weeks. But you didn't like it when someone else took the initiative to train me. I have been using iNews and all other software for two days. Today will be my third day, and you somehow expect me to be an expert on it. There are people in this newsroom who have been using it for years and still aren't experts." The EP, visibly flustered, insisted on his decision. I went to my desk and contacted the bureau chief, who was in Istanbul, and he assured me he would handle it.

To my dismay, my daily salary was reduced from £200 to £150 without my consent. The newsroom atmosphere had turned hostile. I began recording my interactions with the EP and management as I no longer had faith in TRT World. The EP's attempts to undermine me were relentless, likely influenced by knowledge of my father's criticism of British foreign policy in Bosnia. This would be made clear to me a few days later.

The bureau chief had no control over the bureau, with the EP making all significant decisions. When I attempted to increase my workdays, HR claimed that British law prohibited freelancers from working five days a week, yet an inexperienced English freelancer and a Turkish freelancer were working full-time five days a week. When I raised the issue, they told me she was Turkish. "Oh, so that makes it acceptable. Right!" I retorted. As a British citizen, I found myself with fewer rights in the UK than a Turkish output producer. As for the Englishman, well, he was English. The double standards and blatant discrimination were apparent.

I was also passed over for the DPE role, which was instead offered to a Turkish output producer. But I didn't expect to get it anyway. Following this, she began bullying and harassing me, emboldened by the EP's tacit approval. The bureau chief had inappropriately disclosed my friendship with Omer to the EP and others, which led to further alienation and hostility in the newsroom.

The bureau's incompetence was astounding. They made several glaring errors, such as not knowing who Martina Navratilova was. Then a news package provided incorrect information about Mitrovica, Kosovo. When I tried to correct these mistakes, the EP dismissed my concerns, reflecting a disturbing disregard for accuracy and professionalism and accusing me of criticising my colleagues. I looked at him in utter disbelief, both for his reaction and his reply. Was it not better to correct or stop airing false information? Or was editorial policy to broadcast inaccuracies? Having worked in the media, I always triple-checked any information I put out. It was bewildering that this so-called EP reacted as if I were at fault. The lack of care and responsibility for false information was shocking. When I later mentioned this to a Turkish senior producer, she responded, "We don't have experts on the Western Balkans, so you get anyone approving the package, even when they have no clue what they are approving."

The discrimination escalated, making my work environment unbearable. The Turkish Program Editor's refusal to communicate in English during critical moments, especially on the fact that Turks in the newsroom didn't know the difference between East and West Jerusalem, further underscored the exclusionary practices at the channel. I continued to seek other job opportunities, as the hostility and unprofessionalism reached intolerable levels.

On one occasion, I was in the bureau chief's office when he said, "Omer told me I can do whatever I want with you." By then, I had a strong sense that my time at the channel was coming to an end, though I wasn't sure how soon. So, I decided not to hold back. I looked him straight in the eye and said, "Who do you think you are? Do you really believe you can do whatever you want? Just because of my father's article, do you and EP think you can mistreat me? Do you think you have some sort of power over me? I am not someone you can exploit. Maybe in Türkiye that might be acceptable, but here, we have laws."

In another instance, when a new show addressing Islamophobia was in development, I was informed that a Turkish woman was being trained as the producer, despite her lack of experience. They suggested I take on a researcher role instead. I pointed out that I had experience as a series producer and proposed that I produce the show while the Turkish woman could serve as the researcher. However, the response was that despite acknowledging my qualifications, they felt the Turkish woman had more of a claim to the producer role due to her being Turkish at a Turkish channel. Mind boggling! With that response, even if they had made a formal offer of a researcher role, I would have turned it down.

In the days that followed, the discrimination and bullying I faced at TRT World intensified, and my frustration with the job grew to an extreme level. I was actively seeking employment elsewhere because their behaviour was inexcusable, yet they acted with an unrestrained sense of entitlement.

One day, after completing my work for Newshour, I went to the restroom. Upon my return, the Turkish Program Editor reprimanded me for allegedly leaving work unfinished. I responded, "I completed all the tasks assigned to me." She insisted otherwise. I remember another Program Editor laughing and remarking that the EP's puppet was undermining me.

Although she remained silent and didn't acknowledge it directly, she clearly heard the comment and made a point to avoid any further interaction. Her reaction made it obvious that she was complicit in the environment of abuse and favouritism.

Despite my efforts, I was eventually phased out, with my hours given to an English freelancer. The EP's decision was clearly influenced by discriminatory motives, as my attempts to address these issues were met with indifference or outright hostility. Their oversight in failing to remove me from the WhatsApp group proved advantageous. I deliberately remained in the group because it continued to provide a steady stream of evidence for months after my departure. This persisted despite, some months earlier, the Istanbul-based head of news sending an irate email to program editors, instructing them to remove former staff/freelancers from such groups. The inadvertent access to these ongoing conversations offered valuable insights and documentation long after my official exit from the broadcaster.

My time at TRT World ended in February 2023, without any formal explanation for the termination of my freelance engagement. The British establishment's resistance to my presence in the UK media industry was palpable, as they leveraged all means to oust me. The EP's discriminatory practices were blatant yet went unchecked by the channel.

Reflecting on my experience, it was clear that TRT World was rife with unprofessionalism, discrimination, and a toxic work culture. Despite my credentials and dedication, I was subjected to unwarranted hostility and bias.

During this time, I reached out to my father's former editor, Dr Latic, to inquire about the period when my father was writing for *Ljiljan* and how our phone had been bugged due to his contributions. Understanding those details was important to me, especially as my own career continued to face challenges in the UK. Dr Latic explained, "We were closely monitored by various spy networks and embassies, particularly your father, who critically analysed the deceitful policies of the English, especially under John Major and Douglas Hurd. These two will be remembered as shameful accomplices in the aggression against Bosnia and Herzegovina, as well as the genocide and joint criminal enterprise perpetrated by the Chetniks and Ustashas against our Bosniak people. Meanwhile, François Mitterrand and the Russians enabled this tragic situation in every possible way."

As I continued to reach out, prominent diplomats and editors confirmed the injustices faced by my family. Emails poured in, reinforcing what I already knew. I remain grateful to those who had the courage to speak the truth and acknowledge the ongoing abuse that affects Mama and me.

UNCHECKED POWER

Still looking for a job in June 2023, I was in my living room, watching the UK's Channel 4 News with Jackie Long. She was interviewing Tariq Ali,[24] a renowned left-wing campaigner and author. Ali was articulating his experiences in a clear English accent. His narrative felt incredibly personal, as if he were describing my own story. He revealed that fourteen undercover officers had spied on him for nearly six decades. He referenced a report that indicated there was no reason for the surveillance to have continued past October 1968. Despite this, neither the Conservative nor Labour parties questioned senior police officers about these operations.

The political machinations against him proved largely ineffective, but the situation took a sinister turn when lies were made up that even the judge in the published report declared as lies. The judge's ruling not only vindicated him to some degree but also exposed the unsavoury tactics employed by those who sought to discredit him. The incident left a bitter taste, highlighting the often murky intersection of politics, media, and justice. It served as a sobering reminder of the vulnerability of individuals in the face of coordinated smear campaigns, even when the truth is eventually brought to light.

Ali recounted an incident from the 1990s when someone approached him during a walk in Hampstead. The individual revealed that his wife, who worked at Government Communications Headquarters in Cheltenham, had been monitoring Ali's calls. The surveillance, which included listening to personal moments such as breaking up with a partner and his daughter crying at night, was so distressing that it led her to tell her bosses she had not signed up for that sort of work and chose to resign. Ali emphasised that the intrusion into personal lives was often more damaging than any political surveillance because it was more personal and invasive.

Ali's words resonated deeply with me. For the first time in a long time, I felt a sense of being seen. A sense that Mama and I were not the only ones, that this happened to others too. Mama and I had experienced similar violations, feeling isolated and victimised by the British establishment. The confirmation of Ali's surveillance underscored that our experience was not unique but part of a broader unjust practice. Although we were not political activists, we were targeted because of our connection to a man—my father—who had criticised British foreign policy.

I sat in front of the TV remembering how I had written to the UK's political leaders, including former prime ministers and foreign ministers, who repeatedly showed indifference to the detailed letters I sent them. The Foreign Office under the Conservative party claimed that the high-ranking official who had threatened Mama and I no longer worked there, thus absolving the British government of responsibility. But this official was an employee of the Foreign Office when he initiated his campaign of abuse against us. Additionally, he was an undercover MI6 officer in Bosnia, and there is no evidence that he ever left the agency. Even if he did, roles directly associated with the Foreign Office are rarely abandoned entirely, meaning he would still be effectively connected to the department. This implicated both the Foreign Office and the broader government in his actions.

In 2020, the Investigatory Powers Tribunal revealed that MI6 may have unilaterally assumed the power to authorise agents to commit crimes in the UK—potentially without any legal basis or limits on the crimes they can commit.[25] This empowered the high-ranking FCO official to blacklist me from employment, bully and harass Mama and me, and bug our communications without any repercussions.

The British establishment's actions against us seemed driven by a relentless vendetta. The persistent harassment and surveillance were inexplicably cruel, especially considering my father's critical writing about British foreign policy.

Our attempts to seek justice were consistently stonewalled. The police and other authorities offered no support, leaving us to fend for ourselves. Despite these challenges we persevered, installing our own security measures and trying to live our lives amidst the constant threats.

The level of lawbreaking and unethical behaviour we've endured is astonishing. Our lives were invaded due to my father's critical writings and disturbing behaviour by the high-ranking FCO official.

The British establishment operates with a medieval brutishness that is rotten to the core. Their freedom to punish people is not only sadistic but seems driven by a perverse enjoyment in others' suffering. They embody the worst aspects of humanity. Even after my father's death the harassment continued, revealing a pathological need to control and suppress dissent. This medieval-like brutality seems intent on punishing us indefinitely.

Their efforts to sabotage my professional life have been relentless. Moving from media to political analysis, I face continued obstruction. Their fear of my work and insights is baffling. Recently, I was forced to take a freelance job far beneath my qualifications, yet I remain determined to control my future and professional path, refusing to let them dictate my life. The ordeal we've faced indicates a deeply flawed and vindictive system, and its unchecked power and lack of accountability pose a threat to anyone who dares to criticise its actions. Our struggle for justice continues, fuelled by the belief that we must expose the truth and hold those responsible accountable.

The story of Tariq Ali and others like him is a testament to the pervasive nature of surveillance and harassment in the UK. Our fight is far from over, but every acknowledgment of these injustices brings us closer to justice. Our perseverance against the odds is a testament to our resilience and determination to reclaim our lives from those who seek to destroy them.

EXPOSING HYPOCRISY

The war between Russia and Ukraine showed no signs of ending, as US President Joe Biden and his State Department seemed determined to prolong that war with a misplaced hope of toppling Putin, an objective they knew full well was unlikely to be realised. The West often perceives itself as superior yet lacks a true understanding of other cultures and political systems. In their attempts to undermine Putin, they have inadvertently reinforced his position and that of his allies, while diminishing their own influence. Last October, my long-awaited peer-reviewed monograph on Russia's interference in Bosnia's internal security was published in the US as part of a special Russia-focused issue.

Bosnia was experiencing its worst crisis since 1992. The German High Representative, Christian Schmidt, who had strong ties to Croatia, illegally imposed electoral reform just as the polls closed on the October 2022 elections. Bosniaks, the majority, were now treated as if they had no power in their own country. The Croats, a minority who had ethnically cleansed Bosniaks during the war, were now in charge. This change was supported by the Biden administration and the unelected British Prime Minister Rishi Sunak who did not have a mandate to make such a decision. Although I expected such actions from the British government, given their past attempts to partition Bosnia during the war, I was surprised by Biden's support, considering how supportive he was of Bosnia during the 1990s war. But his support largely stemmed from the relentless efforts of key figures such as Senator Joe Lieberman, Senator McCain, and Senator Dole, who were the driving force in American politics behind ending the war. Biden saw Bosnia and these influential senators as a chance to elevate his own profile. Now, given that he had achieved his career goals, I shouldn't have expected him to maintain any dedication to Bosnia. He was not only the worst president in terms of foreign policy, acting in a malevolent manner that has also contributed to weakening the US on the international stage, but his administration also made America an unappealing place to live, leading me to completely lose interest in residing there.

I continued to write and publish abroad about the crisis in Bosnia, especially highlighting how Biden and Sunak's actions played into Russia's hands, allowing them to exploit the new electoral reform to further destabilise Bosnia. But even Putin hasn't done as much damage to Bosnia as Biden, Sunak, and Schmidt did. I pitched an article to TRT World digital in Istanbul, which they initially accepted. When I submitted the article, they chose not to publish it, claiming that Russian President Vladimir Putin had never explicitly supported Bosnian Serb leader Milorad Dodik. I was astonished and reread the email multiple times to ensure I understood correctly. I had for years by that point written about Russia's continuous interference in not only Bosnia but the entire

Western Balkans, and there was overwhelming evidence to prove this if they didn't want to take my word for it.

TRT World's producer also claimed that Montenegro had never committed war crimes in Bosnia. I countered by pointing out that Serbia and Montenegro were one country during the Yugoslav wars and jointly committed war crimes in Croatia and Bosnia. I failed to mention that since 2006, Montenegro had held eight trials for war crimes committed in Bosnia and Herzegovina, Croatia, and Kosovo.

Additionally, the producer stated that "While Covic did employ Bosniaks under difficult conditions, it is important to clarify that these were workers in his own company and not individuals held in concentration camps." But several regional outlets reported on the testimonies of survivors and have even published documents revealing that Covic, a leader of the HDZ, requested Heliodrom detainees to be assigned to work for his company.[26] In the Heliodrom, prisoners endured both mental and physical abuse. Guards frequently beat them, especially as tensions between Bosnia and Croatia intensified, and there were instances where guard dogs were unleashed on the inmates. Some prisoners were transported to Mostar for forced labour, including tasks such as digging trenches, constructing military fortifications, and collecting the bodies of deceased HVO soldiers. In the most extreme cases, they were coerced into walking in front of HVO forces as human shields. The war in Bosnia and Herzegovina lasted from April 6, 1992, to December 14, 1995, and Herzegovina, like the rest of Bosnia, witnessed brutalities against Bosniak civilians. Therefore, these individuals were not workers but prisoners of war.

With unwavering conviction, I decided to expose the channel's biased comments and my rebuttals on my X account, including damning evidence of Covic's signature requesting prisoners from Heliodrom. The response from fellow Bosnians was overwhelmingly supportive.

Some media figures, lacking a deep understanding of the historical complexities of the Bosnian War, attempted to downplay or obscure the events that led to genocide. The narrative pushed by certain individuals at TRT World reflects the subjective editorial choices of its team rather than any official government stance. This team often seems influenced by Western perspectives that have historically shown little empathy for the Bosniak community, leading to decisions driven more by personal bias than by factual integrity.

I approached TRT World's editorial content with low expectations, but I was still shocked by their blatant disregard for decency and their poor understanding of the Bosnian War. Their baseless assumptions and defence of the indefensible were startling. At the very least, they could have done some basic research before spreading misinformation.

Now, it's time for Bosnia to reclaim its narrative and stand firm on its own historical and cultural foundations. We are not a buffer zone between East and West, nor a playground for foreign powers. We are Bosnia—richly diverse, intricately complex, occasionally divided, but always distinctly ourselves.

Our future must embrace unity within diversity, honouring our complex heritage while forging a shared path forward. We must resist those who attempt to simplify our identity for their own agendas, whether they are nationalist politicians within our borders or foreign entities seeking influence.

Bosnia's history has been shaped by four distinct cultural eras. Simply walking through our towns, wandering through our forests, or standing beside our lakes and springs allows one to feel the weight of history, as though living through centuries of empire and change. And when the embers of conflict finally cooled, Bosnia would rise again under new leadership from another empire until one day that empire would be her own.

The Bosnia I envision is one that honours every aspect of its heritage while confidently charting its own course in today's world. It is a Bosnia that stands tall among nations, not as a client state or a historical footnote but as a unique and invaluable member of the global community.

This is the undeniable truth about Bosnia, a truth that no amount of propaganda or historical revisionism can erase. It is a truth we must assert boldly and proudly, standing against anyone who tries to define us on their terms rather than our own.

A JOURNEY THROUGH FIRE AND HOPE

As I pen the final words of this book, my heart swells with a tempest of emotions. Five long years have passed since I first started writing, each day a battle to pour my soul onto these pages. This isn't just a story, it's the raw, beating heart of my chaotic life, an odyssey thrust upon me by forces beyond my control.

This book has been my child, my confidant, my tormentor. I've nurtured it through sleepless nights and tear-stained days, wearing every hat from writer to editor to therapist. When my publishing editor finally took my hand, guiding me through the labyrinth of my past, it was like stepping through a portal. I watched myself grow, change, and evolve, leaping over hurdles and smashing through barriers that once seemed impenetrable. This wasn't just writing, it was rebirth.

Now, as I write this conclusion, the sun caresses my face just as it did on that fateful day in April 1992 when my world shattered and I became a refugee. A gentle breeze whispers through the leaves outside, a stark contrast to the turmoil in my heart. But now, instead of fleeing in terror, I sit near a window in the living room of the London home I share with

Mama, crafting the final chapter of my story, worlds away from the girl I once was.

The world outside my window is a stark reminder that the struggles I've faced are far from unique. Desperate souls risk everything to cross the English Channel, many of whom are swallowed by the merciless sea. In Ukraine, war rages on, fuelled by politicians who view human lives as mere collateral damage in their quest for power and profit. The Middle East bleeds as Gaza and Lebanon face annihilation at the hands of Benjamin Netanyahu's regime. Israeli civilians suffer too; every life lost, regardless of faith or number, is a scar on humanity's conscience.

When will they learn? The hollow cry of "Never Again" rings false, seemingly applicable only to those of the right religious affiliation. In Bosnia, we were treated as children of a lesser god. And now, as I survey the global landscape, I realise with a heavy heart that I've never known a world without war raging somewhere.

We refugees are not statistics. We are dreamers, lovers, fighters, complex souls thrust into impossible situations. Our journey is one of unimaginable loss and trauma, forced to abandon everything we've ever known. If nations are so eager to sow chaos abroad, they must be prepared to shelter those fleeing the storm they've created. Seeking asylum is not a privilege but a fundamental human right, enshrined in international law and morality. Governments have a moral and legal obligation to provide protection to those fleeing persecution.

Given a chance, we can bring vibrant colour to the canvas of our new homes. We are doctors, engineers, artists, but more than that, we are human beings deserving of dignity, family, and the opportunity to rebuild. Many of us are highly skilled professionals, eager to apply our expertise and work ethic in our adopted homes. Language training, access to education, and the right to work are crucial elements for successful integration and self-sufficiency. Yet, in my case, it seems the British establishment has chosen to view these principles as subject to abuse.

The West, blinded by its colonial hangover, fails to learn as people flood the streets demanding justice for the oppressed. I'm reminded of a poignant quote that cuts to the core of our existence: "Us immigrant kids will always be too Eastern for the West, and too Western for the East, our identities will forever remain in disarray." It's a beautiful, aching truth that encapsulates the limbo I've felt in the UK, never quite belonging, always straddling invisible borders.

Although I wish the war in Bosnia had never happened, I find myself grateful that it didn't occur in today's polarized world. I shudder to think of the fate that would have befallen Bosnia and our people if the current crop of politicians had been in power then. I fear we would have shared the tragic fate of Palestine, our predominantly Muslim population left to its own demise as the British Conservatives aided the EU in extinguishing Muslim life in Europe.

Despite the hardships, I find myself filled with gratitude. I'm thankful for those who guided me toward valuable experiences, particularly my grant from the United States army. I'm grateful for Mama's and my good health, and our ability to navigate a country that seems intent on breaking our spirit. We remain strong and steadfast despite the harsh barriers thrown in our way.

I am profoundly grateful for Mama, the unwavering pillar of strength in my life. Her support has been a lifeline infused with a love that knows no bounds. With her by my side, I have weathered the fiercest storms, finding solace in her nurturing embrace as we navigated the tumultuous waves of life together.

Through laughter and tears, we have shared countless moments that have woven the fabric of our bond even tighter. I can still recall those times when we rolled out our yoga mats, despite the cheeky t-shirt I saw in Bond Street that boldly proclaimed, "Yoga kills." In those moments we found joy and connection, even amidst the chaos.

Mama's love and dedication have been my guiding light, illuminating my path during the darkest of times. Her unwavering belief in me has carried me through the challenges I faced. Together, we have built a sanctuary of support and resilience, a testament to the power of love and family. I am endlessly thankful for her presence in my life—a true blessing that I cherish every day.

My heart swells with appreciation for my publisher and editor, who have taken my complicated life story and helped me transform it into a book. This is my story, born of my determination to succeed, but it was the direction and acceptance of my publisher and editor that helped shape it into a publishable work I've had to rewrite three times, ready for a launch in the market that is surpassing the West in its development, innovations, and opportunities.

When my memoir makes its way into the world, I dare to hope that it will finally end the witch-hunt against Mama and me, allowing us to live our lives as we should have been able to all along. I dream of securing a solid job in foreign affairs, where I'm judged not by my father's writing but by my own merit and the wealth of experience I have to offer, all gained outside of the UK.

My heart belongs to foreign policy; it was my first love and will be my last. I envision a future beyond the UK where I can contribute meaningfully to this field while also maintaining a steady stream of writing for various publications. The path ahead may be uncertain, but I face it with the same resilience and determination that has carried me through the storms of my past.

As I conclude this chapter of my life, I hope that the world will look beyond the labels and statistics. See the human faces behind the refugee crisis, the individual stories of loss, courage, and hope. But we are not so different from those that never fled their home in terror. We simply had the misfortune of being born in a place torn apart by forces beyond our control.

Let my story serve as a testament to the indomitable human spirit, a reminder that even in the darkest of times, hope can flourish. May it inspire the reader to stand up for justice, to welcome the stranger, and to fight for a world where "Never Again" truly means never again for all people, regardless of their race, religion, or country of origin.

As the sun sets on this chapter of my life, I look to the horizon with cautious optimism. The journey has been long and fraught with challenges, but it has also been filled with moments of profound beauty and unexpected kindness. I carry with me the lessons of my past, the strength of my heritage, and the dreams of a brighter future, not just for myself but for all those who find themselves adrift in a world that too often turns its back on the vulnerable.

My story is far from over. I yearn for the opportunity to meet with the British Prime Minister, yet a shadow of doubt lingers in my heart, whispering that this moment may never arrive. The British government must confront its moral obligation to acknowledge and rectify the human rights abuses inflicted upon Mama and me. It is imperative that they take responsibility and work diligently to mend the wounds caused by their actions. The weight of injustice cannot be ignored. It demands action, compassion, and a commitment to restoring dignity to our lives.

This book is my testament, my battle cry, my lullaby. It's for every soul adrift in a world that too often turns its back on compassion. May these words be a beacon, illuminating the shared humanity that binds us all, refugee and citizen alike.

Endnotes

1. Cohen, Philip J. (1996). *Serbia's Secret War: Propaganda and the Deceit of History*. Texas A&M University Press
2. Ibid
3. CIA Intelligence Report, "The Military Role of the Serbian Interior Ministry in the Yugoslav Conflict" DCI Interagency Balkan Task Force, October 26, 1995
4. A Chetnik refers to a member of a Serbian nationalist guerrilla force that emerged during World War II, primarily associated with the Yugoslav Army in the Fatherland, led by General Dragoljub Mihailović. The term "Chetnik" saw a revival during the Yugoslav Wars in the 1990s, where various paramilitary groups invoked Chetnik symbolism and ideology, often associated with Serbian nationalism and military actions against non-Serb populations.
5. Muhamed Jusic, "Bosnia and Herzegovina again stands at a crossroad" *Arab News,* March 1, 2022
6. Stephen Engelberg, "Degree Varies as Arabs Assist Bosnia's Muslims" *The New York Times International*, Sunday, August 23, 1992, pp15
7. Vernon Bogdanor, "Srebrenica: the silence over Britain's guilt must be ended" *The Guardian*, 12 July, 2012
8. Patricia Wynn Davies & Annika Savill, "Thatcher demands the arming of Bosnia: 'Massacre of innocents' must end; UN warns that food supplies will run out in days" *Independent*, UK, Tuesday 13 April, 1993
9. William Tuohy, "BALKANS: Thatcher Appeal on Bosnia Stirs War of Words: Christopher describes her comments

as 'emotional.' But her views have support from some Western officials" *Los Angeles Times*, April 16, 1993
10 Ibid
11 Richard Norton-Taylor, "US used Islamists to arm Bosnia" *The Guardian*, UK, April 21, 2022
12 Ibid
13 Wiebes, Cees (2003). *Intelligence and the War in Bosnia, 1992–1995: Volume 1 of Studies in intelligence history*. LIT Verlag. p. 195. ISBN 9783825863470.
14 Embassy of the United Arab Emirates, Washington DC, the UAE-US Cooperation, Security
15 Christoph Marcinkowski; Constance Chevallier-Govers; Ruhanas Harun (2011). *Malaysia and the European Union: Perspectives for the Twenty-first Century*. LIT Verlag Münster. pp. 41–. ISBN 978-3-643-80085-5
16 Muhamed Jusic, "Bosnia and Herzegovina again stands at a crossroad" *Arab News*, March 1, 2022
17 Hamza Karcic, "How Bob Dole saved Bosnia on Capitol Hill" *Foreign Policy*, December 6, 2021
18 United Nations, "UN World Court acquits Serbia of genocide in Bosnia; finds it guilty of inaction" February 26, 2007
19 Robert Fisk, "Europe has a troublingly short memory over Serbia's Aleksander Vucic" *Independent*, May 14, 2016; Vucic: kill one Serb and we will kill 100 Muslims
20 United Nations International Criminal Tribunal for the former Yugoslavia: Landmark Case - "In a number of landmark judgements, the Tribunal advanced the development of international justice in the realm of gender crimes by enabling the prosecution of sexual violence as a war crime, a crime against humanity and genocide."

21 Ibid
22 *Sarajevo Times*, "Brammertz: " It has been proven that it was not a Civil War, but an International Conflict," June 1, 2023
23 Hamza Yusuf, "The British Media Has an Islamophobia Problem" *Tribune*, November 30, 2021
24 Jackie Long, "Police Special Demonstration Squad inquiry: 'I was spied on for almost 60 years', says author and historian" UK's Channel 4 News, June 29, 2023
25 Committee on the Administration of Justice "MI6 unilaterally assumed power to break law on UK soil, tribunal reveals," December 16, 2020
26 Una Hajdari, "Bosnia war survivors outraged by plans to turn torture site into army museum" Euronews, 7 April 2023, and "Dokumenti u posjedu Tužilaštva u Hagu kompromitiraju Dragana Čovića" Otisak.ba, 30 March 2017.

Acknowledgements

This journey, though long and often challenging, has been immeasurably enriched by the remarkable people who have walked alongside me.

To my mother: Your steadfast support, endless patience, and steadfast belief in me have been my anchor. Thank you for answering countless questions, for sharing your wisdom with such gentleness, and for being my guiding light in our shared pursuit of justice. This book is as much yours as it is mine, and I am eternally grateful for everything you have given me.

I want to express my heartfelt gratitude to my publisher, for her invaluable support and guidance throughout the publication process. Her expertise and dedication have significantly enhanced this work, and I am truly grateful for her partnership in sharing my story.

To my editor: Your skill and insight helped me navigate the depths of my past, pulling together memories and words with such care and precision. You didn't just edit my manuscript, you taught me how to write a book. Thank you.

To the entire team at The Dreamwork Collective: the copy editor whose careful attention made the pages seamless;

the gifted designer who created the cover; the meticulous typesetter; and everyone else who contributed to bringing this project to life—your hard work and dedication have not gone unnoticed.

To Peter: You were one of the first to read this book outside of my publishing team, and I am deeply grateful for your time and comments. Thank you.

Thank you to Winnie, Aizhanat, and the unforgettable Brussels crew—Lana, David, Nuala—and to all the teachers and mentors: Your laughter, lessons, and light have enriched my journey in ways I will always treasure.

About the Author

Nadina, a Bosnian-born author, fled her homeland as a child during the war, finding refuge in the UK. Her diverse career spans journalism and foreign policy analysis, with a particular focus on Russian geopolitics. Her expertise has been recognised with a grant from the US Army War College's Strategic Studies Institute. Nadina's journalistic background includes work for CNBC and Fox Business, as well as contributions to Al Jazeera English, Middle East Eye, and the *Journal of Peace and War Studies*. From an early age, Nadina demonstrated a knack for commentary, appearing on Channel 4 News at 15 to discuss the end of the Bosnian War. At 17, she interviewed Guns N' Roses' Slash. Beyond her professional pursuits, she harbours a deep passion for music, cinema, travel, and photography.

About the Publisher

The Dreamwork Collective is a print and digital publisher sharing diverse voices and powerful stories with the world. Dedicated to the advancement of humanity, we strive to create books that have a positive impact on people and on the planet. Our hope is that our books document this moment in time for future generations to enjoy and learn from, and that we play our part in ushering humanity into a new era of heightened creativity, connection, and compassion.

www.thedreamworkcollective.com

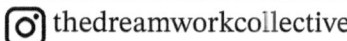 thedreamworkcollective

www.ingramcontent.com/pod-product-compliance
Lightning Source LLC
LaVergne TN
LVHW041752060526
838201LV00046B/974